MW01061584

PRAISE FOR

Reaching *for* Beautiful

"The most enduring books write us and touch on the common human journey. *Reaching for Beautiful* is such a book. What Sally McQuillen endured in bringing a child into the world only to lose him decades later holds lessons for us all. Her brave and tender story will make any reader value life and our chance to be here more."

—**Mark Nepo, *New York Times* #1 bestselling author of**
You Don't Have to Do It Alone* and *The Half-Life of Angels

"*Reaching for Beautiful* is not just for someone who has lost a child, or has loved a child, it's for anyone who has loved at all. McQuillen writes with the voice of a poet, lyrically, as well as straight to the heart. Her story is both a heartbreaking and a heart-opening must-read."

—**Kristen Moeller, MS, literary agent and author of**
What Are You Waiting For?

"McQuillen is unafraid to share the roller coaster ride that is family addiction as she grapples with grief in *Reaching for Beautiful*. As a therapist who helps clients who have been impacted by addiction, her loss is particularly poignant."

—**Sukey Forbes, bestselling author of *The Angel in My Pocket***

"This tender story of a mother navigating the loss of her extraordinary son is written with mercy and wisdom. Mercy toward herself as a loving mom who will always miss the physical presence of her beloved son. And wisdom as she shares the journey of spiritual awakening that her son's spirit takes her on. These mysteries bring her to the truths we all seek about what is essential in life. Only love. What a wonderful book for anyone wondering if grief will have the last word."

—**Sue Frederick, author of *Bridges to Heaven:***
True Stories of Loved Ones on the Other Side

Reaching
for
Beautiful

Reaching for Beautiful

*A Memoir of
Loving and Losing
a Wild Child*

Sally McQuillen

SHE WRITES PRESS

Published 2025
Printed in the United States of America
Print ISBN: 978-1-64742-860-0
E-ISBN: 978-1-64742-861-7
Library of Congress Control Number: 2024923008

For information, address:
She Writes Press
1569 Solano Ave #546
Berkeley, CA 94707

Interior design by Stacey Aaronson

She Writes Press is a division of SparkPoint Studio, LLC.

Christopher—I hope the power of my love for you punches into your dimension like a firework. Thank you for shining so bright you've become the light in me. You make my life as your mother so beautiful.

Everything is beautiful and I am so sad.
This is how the heart makes a duet of
wonder and grief. The light spraying
through the lace of the fern is as delicate
as the fibers of memory forming their web
around the knot in my throat. The breeze
makes the birds move from branch to branch
as this ache makes me look for those I've lost
in the next room, in the next song, in the laugh
of the next stranger, in the very center, under
it all, what we have that no one can take
away and all that we've lost face each other.
It is there that I'm adrift, feeling punctured
by a holiness that exists inside everything.
I am so sad and everything is beautiful.

"Adrift," Mark Nepo

*I*t is a chilly Sunday morning in January. I'm drawn down to the living room by the warmth of the fire. I settle into the loveseat facing the fireplace, wrap a blanket around my shoulders, and take a sip of my Starbucks. Christmas is behind us, but I haven't yet taken down our decorations, wanting the kids to enjoy them while they are home. I look over at our five stockings lying empty on the bench by the hearth and study each one closely. My mother's needlework of a snowman for my "baby" William, 16, who's sound asleep in his room, of a pink pile of presents for my only girl Caroline, 19, currently visiting her college boyfriend in St. Louis, and of a Santa for my firstborn Christopher, 21, who's home from college and off at his friend Simon's lake house.

I pick up Chris's stocking, admiring Grammy's stitchery. Santa is making a list and checking it twice. I chuckle to myself, *Naughty or nice?* and think about how, with Chris, it's a toss-up and a little bit of both! I rub my fingers along the black velvet backing and notice that our Christmas tree, laden with too many ornaments, has begun to sag.

The tree is looking less fresh than it did a week ago. I'm going to have to take it down before it collapses. Soon its lonely skeleton will have to be tossed to the curb. My favorite ornaments take me down memory lane—the hand-made cut-out snowflakes and glitter-covered glass balls look a little more faded with each passing year, but I cherish each one and hope they last forever. I step over to the corner of the room to sweep my hand across the wood floor underneath the tree, collecting sharp prickles of pine needles in my palm. I squeeze them and inhale what little of their scent remains.

My husband's phone rings, and I hear him answer from the kitchen.

"What do you mean *missing*? Who is this?" Joe's loud voice interrupts the quiet. My heart begins to pound from inside my ears. I can't see Joe from the living room, but I'm on alert. "They probably just ended up at some girl's house near the lake," he tells the person on the line. But then I hear him say, as if in disbelief, "Wait, how many kids are missing?" He pauses. "Four boys took out a canoe? I'm on my way." My heart pounds louder.

I race to the kitchen, where I watch Joe slurp a spoonful of cereal into his mouth. I'm incredulous. Why isn't he already out the door? He sets the bowl down, heads to grab his coat, and tells me, "Simon's dad called to tell me Chris and three other boys took a canoe out last night. They left their phones in the boathouse. I can't imagine what those knuckleheads got up to. I'm going to head up and find out."

Joe has come to Christopher's rescue so many times. I guess he thinks this time is like all the others—that there will be an explanation for this. Maybe the kids canoed across the lake to a nearby bar and passed out somewhere. Who knows. With Chris, anything is possible. Joe hurries out the door to take the hour drive up north to Wisconsin from Illinois, reassuring me that he'll track them down. Chris went up yesterday to spend the night, and we're anticipating him home this afternoon. A bunch of guys were gathering at Simon's lake house on Lake Beulah. My brother Rick has a little summer house there, too, but he rarely gets up to it from Chicago.

I feel unsteady and start to pace. I wander from room to room without seeing. Uneasiness weakens me. I'm faint and can't stop wringing my hands. I rapidly roll my thumb in circles against one of my gold rings while trying to think. I'm clenching my teeth and have stopped breathing.

I'm as afraid as I have ever been.

Because I know.

I can't remember ever not being afraid. I can trace my fear back to childhood, when my dad's presence could set alarms in my highly sensitive nervous system. He walks through the side kitchen door after work, heads straight to the liquor cabinet, and reaches for a bottle. He can't see me, but I can see him through the banister slats as I peer down from the top of our staircase. I watch him pour brown liquid into a crystal glass and gulp it down before I tiptoe back to my room and close my bedroom door.

Back in my room, painted robin's egg blue, I open my closet and my brother Charlie, two years younger than me, jumps out—all gangly arms and legs.

I scream, "Dad, Charlie jumped out of my closet again! Tell him to stop scaring me!" I know my mom is busy cleaning up in the kitchen. I wait for my dad, then call out, "Dad, can you help me?"

When he gets upstairs, I point to where, beneath my hanging clothes, it's possible there could be someone else hiding. Instead of reassuring me that it's just my vivid imagination getting the best of me again, he steps into the back of my closet, pulls my clothes aside, and proclaims,

"Sal, the only thing in here is a fruit witch, but she won't hurt you." He cackles as I jump backward. He continues to laugh as he leaves my room.

I close the door behind him, try to get ready for bed, and hope that the green-faced fruit witch lurking in the dark corner of my closet will leave me alone.

Once I became a mom, the seedlings of fear that sprouted in my childhood began to reappear. I was feeding Christopher's new baby sister when I realized it had become too quiet. I turned the house upside down, but Chris was nowhere to be found. I plopped Caroline in the car seat and circled our suburban neighborhood in our minivan, calling his name out the window and asking neighbors to keep an eye out for him. I called the police and tearfully described the blue striped T-shirt and denim shorts he was wearing, his sandy blonde hair, and his big cheeks. My eyes darted back and forth as I gripped the steering wheel. I drove slowly around the block and imagined what it would be like to tell my husband that I'd lost our son.

I couldn't find him anywhere. Back home, I stood outside the car, motionless on the driveway, as if my feet were sinking into the concrete while waiting for the police to arrive. Without a word, neighbors gathered, sensing my alarm. I kept my eyes peeled in the distance.

Suddenly Chris came running around the corner with another little boy and a tall woman hurrying them along, compassionately shaking her head. I ran to him, pulled him against my chest, and squeezed him so hard he groaned. Surprise widened his eyes as he studied me blinking away my tears.

"Mommy, Mommy, I go see Mowrlie!" He stumbled over his words in his excitement to tell me where he'd been. Our neighbor's black Lab had caught Chris's eye. He had followed the dog around the block and into their backyard to play. Chris was always distracted by whatever grabbed his interest—tractors, planes, anything that moved—and wanted the freedom to go after it.

I try to sit down on the floor, but my heart is racing, so I resume pacing. Then it hits me. Maybe Chris will turn up like he did as a little boy. Maybe he and his friends took the canoe out to my brother's place on the other side of the lake. Maybe they found a way to get in and then spent the night there. He'd been there before and thought it was cool that his friend had a place not far from his uncle's.

I'm walking back and forth, talking to myself, not knowing what to do, when William comes upstairs and immediately stops in his tracks.

"Bugs, Dad went up to Wisconsin. Your brother took a canoe out with some friends last night and we don't know where he is. Can you call Uncle Rick and see if, by any chance, Chris ended up there?" I'm too frantic . . . pull out my phone, access Rick's contact info, and hand it over to William. I know this is a stab-in-the-dark attempt to make sense of a senseless situation. Rick doesn't answer, so William leaves a message and then stays close as I call Joe. Joe suggests mentioning it to Simon's dad, too, and gives me his number. He's still en route to the lake, nearing the border of Illinois and Wisconsin.

I reach out to Simon's dad and leave a message. "Hi, it just occurred to me that the boys could have ended up at my brother's. He has a lake house across the lake from you. Just thought you should know. Joe told me you're in touch with your son and everyone who's looking. Please, keep us posted."

William sits next to me on the loveseat, where I try to catch my breath. I am exhaling in short bursts, and I start to feel faint.

Tears begin to fall even though I don't want my youngest to see me like this.

"Mom, it's going to be all right," he says as he pats me gently on the shoulder. "Don't worry, Mom," he pleads. "It's okay." He is scared, too, so I try to calm down for his sake.

"You're right, sweetie. I'm just freaking out. Don't you worry either." It isn't like me to get hysterical. Emotional, yes, but not breathless. My heart is desperate with its knowing, but I berate myself for not having faith that my beloved boy is all right.

Rick calls back. "Sal, I just checked. No one has been to my house. Are you sure there isn't anywhere else he could have gone?"

My heart drops deeper in my chest. I can't speak. The possibility that Chris is safe, that momentary sliver of hope that grants me all I've ever wanted, slips away. Frightened and on autopilot, my words fall flat. I'm faking it. "I'm sure there's some explanation, Rick. I'll keep you posted."

"Yeah Sal, let me know."

I can't get off the phone fast enough. Rick knows me as well as I know myself. He and I have always had a sixth sense when it comes to each other.

William stands by my side, looking helpless as I walk in circles. I am retreating into myself, so he heads back down to his room. Everything gets fuzzy. My thoughts race. Chris wouldn't have hesitated to go on an adventure. If the other kids wanted to go out on a canoe in winter, he would have been all-in. *Ohhhhh sweetheart. Where are you?*

Joe calls, and I pick up before the first ring even comes through. "Do you have Peter's mom's number? We can't get ahold of Peter's parents. Simon's dad isn't calling me back."

He hasn't returned my call, and now he isn't returning Joe's. He must know something.

He tells me he's getting another call and puts me on hold.

When he clicks back over, his voice is softer than usual.

"Honey, that was Simon's uncle. They found an overturned canoe."

My heart sinks as unbearable images of a canoe tipping into the ice and cold take hold.

"The other parents haven't even been contacted. What the *hell is* going on?" Joe says to himself before he hangs up. But I'm not listening.

I fall to the floor, get on my knees, and beg, *GOD, TAKE ME INSTEAD! PLEASE GOD.* My shaking hands reach up to a God I rarely ask for anything. I plead, *just let him be okay. I will give my life for his. It's been a good life. I'm ready. Take me. I will do anything for him to be safe. PLEEASSE!*

Minutes pass like hours as I wait for Joe to get to Wisconsin and let me know that our son is all right. Fear screams in my chest. Rick called my brother Charlie, who lives in the next town, and told him what's happening because the next thing I know, Char runs through the door and is standing at my side. I adore my brother and am reassured by his presence, but the fact that he has arrived here so quickly isn't a good sign. I look up at him from the floor, where I'm still kneeling as Joe calls again. None of them made it, Sal. I hear only the words "He's gone" before my world explodes and my heart shatters.

Visions of my beautiful child and his friends falling from the canoe into an icy-cold lake consume me, and there is nothing but agony and torture. I want to turn back time, save him, go instead. I'm terrified. No longer in my body, thrust into darkness, I cry out. Then I mumble to Joe that I am sorry and begin to hyperventilate. "NOOOOOOOOO, NOOOOO!" I rebel. I'm ranting as my sister-in-law Carolyn arrives. She sits beside me as my brother rubs my back. But I am not here. I'm floating into pitch blackness.

I can't sleep. When I finally succumb, I dreamily relive a moment in time.

I'm in rolled-up jean shorts and a T-shirt, with long, straight blonde hair hanging down my back. My little girl legs and bare feet dangle over a worn seat of wood, tanned arms reach up to the twisted ropes attached to a strong tree. I slip closer and feel the weight of my body held beneath an outstretched branch. I tighten my grip, extend my toes from just above the water, reaching for the deep blue sky, and pull my heels back from bright fluffy clouds to the lake. The afternoon sun reflects in ripples of light across the water. Back and forth, launching higher and higher, enveloped in pure peace, I swing. Letting go with each bend of my knees. A soft breeze whispers across my face as I fly free.

I open one eye and look at my hands. They aren't holding tightly to the ropes of a tree swing. They're clutching the corners of my pillowcase. I'm no longer free. Pain assaults my shoulder blades. My middle-aged hips stick to the mattress. I am gradually waking but can't move.

There is a weight on my sternum, like the heel of a hand pushing my chest beneath my ribs. When did this dark shadow enter my room? How could I have missed its lurking, waiting to pounce against my bones?

My breath quickens in repeated exhales, then stops altogether as I try to get my bearings. My chest tightens. I slowly roll into a fetal position.

Where are you? Where have you gone?

Turn off the dawning.

Wrap me back up in my dreams.

Do not unlock the daylight. Keep me from falling.

Flung from my swing, I tumble down a cliff onto rocks that pierce my skin. My wounds are open and bloody and covered in dust. When I finally land fully awake, I am sobbing.

Nooooo God. Please. No. No. Not my son, so very much alive.

Not my beautiful boy, my beloved child.

You. Cannot. Have. Died.

I 'm plunged into remembering. Every cell of my body feels eviscerated and weak. The dread makes it hard to lift my head from my pillow. I drag myself from bed, smothered in grief, and head downstairs to the loveseat across from the fire. *I hate the cold and so did my baby.* I wrap a soft blanket around my shoulders. I study the ice clinging to the barren trees outside the living room window. I try to keep the haunted images of my child dying at bay as I stare at the trees' stark black arms reaching across the gray winter sky. They seem to be shaking their fists at God.

Why?

My sweet, summer-loving boy is gone. I want to go too. If I'm stuck here in my worst nightmare, I'm going to stay right here by the fire. If I refuse to inhale the frosty air that lies outside my door threatening that bad things can happen, maybe yesterday won't be real.

William must be down in his room, Caroline is on a train coming home from St. Louis, and my mom and stepdad are driving down from Wisconsin. I turn to see the door swing wide open, and Chris's dear friend Avery runs into my arms. She and her mom have walked over from down the block. I haven't seen her for a little while, so I take in the pint-sized twenty-one-year-old college girl who's now sitting in my lap. It feels good to me to gently brush her hair from her face and hug her as we cry together. I'm in shock, but I don't realize it for what it is yet. I'd rather comfort her without having to think about why she's here.

Some of the first to stop by to visit are other mothers in my community who've lost children of their own. Two friends walk in—one lost her son only a short time ago. She enters poised and gives me a quick hug, then the two of them walk back outside and return, tugging a packed cooler between them. She suggests placing a notepad outside the door in case I decide to pace myself with visitors and not answer. She knows that our community will show up in droves, particularly as the news of this tragedy has traveled quickly. I look up at her wizened eyes as tears flow from mine, marveling at her ability to be alive.

Other friends stop in, including a couple who used to be our next-door neighbors. Their son, James, and Chris are the same age. I picture James as a lion and Chris as a bunny for their first Halloween. I see them dancing in their smocked sunsuits on our deck. When Cindy runs toward me sobbing, it scares me. She is the friend who, when I was overwhelmed by our little boys running circles around us, remained unfazed. She is always stoic and rock solid. It must mean this is real, but it can't be. *Where have you gone?* As more people drop by and my mom, who's just appeared, begins to shelve casseroles in the fridge and put flowers into vases, I reply to texts and try as hard as I can to respond graciously to every condolence. This is the only way I know how to be tethered to the earth even though I've entered an abyss.

I want to die. How can I possibly go on living in a world without my son in it? So very much alive, so much excitement for everything he did. My thrill-seeking, sweet boy. How will I survive? Nothing feels the same. I don't know who I am, where I am, where he is. All I can think about is how I'd do anything, give anything, to see him, touch him, hug him again. I scramble for any way to bring him closer, saving every photo that's posted on social media I haven't seen before. I study each one and obsessively ask his friends to send me what they have. A Facebook friend reaches out and suggests I begin writing about my grief. I like to write, even though I've never taken the time to journal, so her idea appeals to me. I take out my phone and begin texting him as if he were here, and it gives me relief.

My world has gone from color to black and white. I can't ever lay my eyes on you again. I'm lost without you calling me Momma. I'm trying to bear it with grace, but I am bereft of innocence, of meaning, of you....

I have always been driven by my feelings. Now, my feelings are *all* I am. I hope writing can become a way to express my yearning. I have never known such an ache. I want to stay connected to my boy. I don't feel him with me, he is out of reach, so I muster faith and focus on all the love that is overflowing from my heart for him. I try to talk to him and hope he hears me.

I got sober a week after I turned twenty-five. I was wild and free-spirited, and my foray into drugs had frightened me enough that I'd landed at an outpatient treatment center for alcoholism. The professionals who assessed me surprised me by insisting I needed their program. When I downplayed how much I drank and explained that I was just there to give up the drugs, they advised that my whole life would need to change—and somehow it did.

Without my high school friends Stacey and Tom, I would never have imagined I'd find myself at a sober dance on a Friday night. They pulled me along. There we were in a church gym at the edge of the city. Still baffled that it was possible to have fun without booze, everyone out on the dance floor seemed to be proving me wrong.

"Sal, I know it feels a bit lame. We're not out at a club, but there are lots of cool people here. And let's face it: you and me and alcohol don't mix," said my pretty friend Stacey, her long blonde hair blown in front of her face by one of the giant fans on the dance floor perimeter.

"Oh hey, there's Joe. Great guy. You've got to meet him." Her blue eyes sparkled as she stood next to me watching everyone dancing all around us.

"How do you know him?" I yelled over Steve Winwood's "Roll with It."

She smiled and turned before heading out on the floor. "He wanted to go out with me, but I just wasn't interested. He's such a nice guy." That was the cue for me to know why she wasn't interested. She tended to favor the "bad boys."

I wasn't interested in dating anyone, but before I knew it, I was meeting Joe, and he was dragging me out into the center of the dance floor. I was self-conscious dancing without having had a few drinks first, but I liked that this guy didn't seem to care what anyone thought. He didn't have rhythm, but he had enthusiasm. He soon became my best friend and, later, my husband.

Joe came from a blue-collar town in Buffalo, and I grew up half blueblood in the suburbs of Chicago. I struggled with depression, while Joe's mantra was "Don't worry. Be happy." I was raised Protestant and Joe was raised Catholic. He has great loyalty to his Irish heritage—and passed this along to our kids.

Joe and I are both more spiritual than religious. We both

believe in a Higher Power, which we call God, but we each define that Higher Power in our own way.

My faith in God has developed over time from being elusive and outside of me into a feeling of love that resides within me and gives me strength. I must call on that faith now. I need to know I can communicate with my son. I need to believe he's okay. I need to know that my world will reattach to its axis.

Family members materialize before us, some of them flying in the very day they hear the news. In the twenty-four hours since I found out my baby is gone, dozens of people have been in and out of the house. Joe and Michael, Christopher's godfather, head out that morning to arrange for the upcoming wake, funeral, and reception. They find a cemetery and pick out a gravestone and casket. I sit the entire time at our farm table in the breakfast room, sorting through stacks of pictures I'd meant to put in albums. I'm numb. My mom sits by my side trying to keep me on task to make selections for the video we'll have at Chris's wake. I get lost in each picture and have trouble staying focused. Things are happening too fast. I wonder where my son has gone and if the ground will emerge beneath my feet. My heart feels ripped from my chest. Looking at pictures, I am flung from a split second of joyful recollection to despair. I try to savor the memories and imprint them on my brain. I don't want to forget anything. I'm afraid of losing my memories too.

While we are downstairs, greeting friends and family and sifting through pictures, Joe returns home from meetings with the priest and the funeral home director. The first thing he does is call up a medium he's seen in the past. Some might think this uncharacteristic of my tough Irish husband, that he would choose to seek solace in something more offbeat, but he is not unacquainted with loss. The youngest of ten children, he has already lost both parents, three of his brothers, two of his sisters, and a niece. He has been comforted by anything that solidifies his belief that Heaven is real.

Joe calls to me to come upstairs. I enter his home office, which used to be Christopher's bedroom before he moved out. The room is still painted royal blue from his childhood. Joe's desk, filing cabinet, and printer don't sync with my memories of this room as Chris's Beatrix Potter nursery followed by his "big boy" room decorated in a coastal theme of lighthouses with a color scheme of red, white, and blue. Joe motions for me to sit down across from him at his desk.

"Remember Nancine?" he asks. "I know you aren't too sure about this stuff, but I have to tell you what she just said." I remembered her from the last time—how she'd somehow known Joe's dad had spent his life working on the railroad. She'd told him his dad was showing her a caboose, which reassured and amazed him. I'd wanted to believe but I was cynical. I'd gone to her myself after my grandfather died, and she'd told me he was in Heaven dancing. That didn't sound like him. Afterward, much later, I did wonder whether she might have been channeling my great-grandfather instead. He'd been known to love to dance. It all seemed too obscure. Just guesswork.

Joe folded his hands out in front of him, dropped his head, and said, "Nancine told me he passed quickly, Sal. She said Chris became distracted by the beauty he discovered on the other side. He didn't consider looking back. He didn't suffer."

I stand up, my chest seizing a bit. I'm not breathing. It is unbearable to think about. I hesitate. "It does sound like him, Bear. I can picture it happening that way. We know he was susceptible to distraction." My voice starts to break as I step into the hall. "Thanks for telling me." I turn to rejoin everyone sorting through photos. I choose to try to believe this version of events.

That afternoon, a news crew descends out front of our home and interviews Joe about the incident resulting in the deaths of four young men. My brothers help write Chris's eulogy. Food, flowers, cards, and gifts are constantly being dropped off, and it takes all I have to try to be present and let myself receive the support pouring in. Joe and I didn't talk about it, but I knew he'd been the one to identify Christopher's body the day before. Chris was the first of the four boys from our community they found. Two other boys were located later in the day. When Joe returned home from Wisconsin, the rescue team was still trying to recover one of the boys. Since they'd recovered my son first, someone sent me a picture of an eagle on a tree overseeing the rescue workers as an attempt to soothe me. It did not yet have that effect. Nor did a doctor friend's insistence that drowning was a peaceful way to go.

If anyone uses the word drowning in my presence, it is extremely unsettling to me. When I hear it, I recoil. I become overwrought and can't bear that it wasn't me instead. That I wasn't there to comfort my child. The hardest part of my horror is to imagine that Christopher was afraid. It is unthinkable to me that three other boys lost their lives when he did. Well beyond what I can absorb, I am strangely comforted that my son was not alone. Mostly, the fact there are other mothers in this excruciating pain is not something I can begin to integrate. I become more and more haunted by the brutal and intermittent images that assault me of my son and three other boys dying. These traumatic interruptions wreak havoc. I fight them off. I don't feel safe and am not able to let myself go where these thoughts take me.

I'm three days into this surreal existence suspended between two worlds. Days pass, but I remain stuck, floating above my own body. Joe and Caroline go alone to see Chris in his open casket at the funeral home before the wake being held that afternoon. They come back, encouraging me to leave it open, telling me that other people will want to see him too. Immediately I am averse to the idea. An open casket service, customary in the Catholic religion, feels strange to me as a Protestant. I never imagined having to make decisions or sign off on what kind of casket or gravestone design there should be. I feel pressured. I tell them I need to see Chris first and then I'll decide.

I know I need to see him. My mom and Rick offer to come with me. When we get to the funeral home, the funeral director approaches me to tell me what a beautiful job was done on my handsome son. Of course every mother sees her children as beautiful. But Christopher was perfect. I don't know what he'll look like now, and I start to shake as we enter the room.

I stop in the back of the room. Mom holds one hand and Rick the other as we sit down on a bench a short distance from my child's body. This is a mother's worst nightmare, but I try to be strong.

I see my baby lying in his best blue suit, and I'm hit by a wave of pain so sharp, it cuts through me. I think I moan as I slowly let go of my mother and brother's hands to approach my son. This couldn't be real. There is no gravity, but I am pulled to kneel before his gorgeous shell of a body.

I look down at him lying there and, as always, he takes my breath away. Yet, his life force isn't there. I don't know where it has gone, but his bright light is no longer present. I will spend the rest of my life trying to connect to his spark. It turns out we are not our bodies. We are the energy inside them. I now see how we place too much emphasis on form, not substance. On our bodies versus our souls. Our essence gives us our light.

A sense of calm descends upon me as I realize his beautiful soul must have gone somewhere. Strangely, my fear disappears. I begin to release the breath I have been holding since he was born. Somehow, I feel like he is all right after all. My worry rises from my own body. It lifts from deep inside where I have always anxiously feared his early departure. I don't have to worry about my wild child anymore. He is in a state of grace beyond my comprehension. I agree with Joe and Caroline that everyone should have the privilege of seeing Chris's body one last time.

three

*I*t has been four days since he left the house. I want to turn back time. If only I could stop the clock at Christmas. Joe and I have just emerged from the basement where I'd stuck my nose into some of Christopher's shirts and found one with a strong hit of his scent—a warm, woodsy boy smell I'll never smell again. I held the shirt close, got lost in it, and then called Joe down to smell it for himself. Sobbing, bereaved, my missing him overwhelms me. There is no one who is anything like my son. His absence throws a blanket over my eyes, saturating my world in blackness.

I head over to the still-sagging Christmas tree and lay down beneath it, just as I did as a little girl each year to look up at the colored lights and dream about what presents might appear underneath it on Christmas morning. Christmas is so magical. I tend to go overboard, and this year, especially, I'm so glad I did. Joe and I usually get last-minute jitters that maybe there won't be enough for each of our kids to open, and this year was Chris's year to be spoiled. Lying here now nine days later, Christmas feels like a lifetime ago.

My favorite tradition has always been filling stockings, and my kids indulge me now that they're older. "Wow Santa, that miniature checkers game is the best!" The first thing Chris did after unwrapping his stocking treasures was to look up at me with his bright green eyes and throw me his Maple Sugar Santa Claus, knowing it's my favorite candy. "Here you go, Momma!" Crackly on the outside, soft and sweet on the inside. It melted on my tongue.

Chris had proudly handed me a wrapped gift—a necklace that he'd picked out and purchased with his own money. Before clasping the silver Tree of Life necklace around my neck, I'd jumped up from the floor where I sat and gave him the biggest hug. I will never take it off. I reach up to touch the silver disc and rub it between my finger and thumb, the same way I have often grabbed our yellow Lab Cassidy's ear at the very softest part. I need soothing, and this helps me not to be so terrified. The tree's sparkly black branches on the necklace are made from hematite. I look it up on my phone. Hematite has grounding properties and can help people connect back to their bodies. *How did you know I'd need this, my precious child?* The strength of a solid trunk dug into the earth with deep roots and its leafy branches reaching for the sun become my talisman. When I flash back to finding out he died, my heart rate increases, my breath catches, and I try to reassure myself that I'm all right even though I'm not.

On this morning, like every morning since my world was rocked, when I wake up, I'm assaulted by the reality of what happened. I would rather be in a state of consciousness the truth can't touch. I realize that I forgot to recite my daily prayer for him the morning of his death, the one I've been reciting for months, ever since he started drinking again. I was planning to read it once I got downstairs, but before I'd had the chance, we received the phone call informing us our son was missing.

Child of Light, I bless You!
I think of You. I pray for You.
But not in terms of what I think you need,
Or what I think you should do or be or express!
I lift my thoughts about you.
I embrace a new vision of you.
I see you as a Child of Light.
I see you guided and directed by an inward
Spirit that leads you unerringly onto the
path that is right for you.
I see you strong and whole.
I see you blessed and prospered.
I see you capable and successful.
I see you free from limitations or bondage of any kind.
I see you as the spiritually perfect being you truly are.
Child of Light, I bless You!

—Martha Smock, *Daily Word*, 1975

I don't know why I waited to read it until after I got out of bed. I'd never waited before. I blame myself for what happened. Magical thinking prompts my mind to wander: *Oh my God, could forgetting to read it right away have caused this to happen?* I'm driving myself crazy. But no, logical me knows he was already gone before I woke up. In fact, I am now waking up at about 3:30 each morning, and I'm filled with an eerie intuition that that is likely the time I lost him. Reciting this prayer has helped reassure me that Christopher was being kept safe by a power greater than me. It helped me feel less driven by the fear that had always stirred my insides when it came to my wild and reckless boy.

Getting up from under the Christmas tree, I begin to wonder if the prayer *has come true*. Just not the way I had in mind. Maybe there is some greater plan beyond my comprehension. Joe, who has endured more than the average amount of loss in his life, is asking whether God betrayed him by taking our beloved son, but I don't think we are being punished. I believe we humans are here on earth to learn and grow, and not everyone is meant to live into old age. Whatever the divine plan is, or my lesson to learn from it, the pain may be too great for me to bear.

I'm not sure what's happening, but I am relying on God like never before. Where else can I turn? Today, I whisper a new prayer: *Please, God, don't let my child have suffered. Don't let him have been afraid. Let him have risen into the warmest rays of bright light. Wrap him up in infinite love.* As I say these words, I try to picture a Heaven I'm not sure exists. I try to imagine handing my boy over to God, an offering of one of my three most prized creations, but it demands too great a sacrifice. Instead, I just want to leap out of my body and reach toward the sky. Is that where Heaven is? Where God is? Where my son's spirit now lives? I want to pull him back to me.

Letting go is an important spiritual teaching. I've let go of alcohol and drugs and tried to turn my life over to God's care. But I don't want to let go of my son. I can't let go of my son. The only way I can let him go is if I know I'll always have him.

On my dresser for forty years has sat Helen Keller's words, "All that we love deeply, becomes a part of us," written in calligraphy on a burnt-edged piece of paper shellacked to a piece of wood that I brought home from summer camp. I hope my son will become a deeper part of me and, at the same time, be set free, my "child of light."

I want Christopher to be safe and comforted. I want to find a way to feel safe and comforted, too, despite my emptiness and desperation. In the past, I sought comfort in alcohol and drugs, but I know those sleepless alcohol- and drug-fueled nights only brought me to false emotional heights and threw me back onto the pavement the morning after. I can't imagine what this would be like if I was still drinking. Although I'm twenty-eight years sober, I still look for ways to escape my feelings. Thankfully, I have not wanted to pick up a drink. I need to find healthy sources of comfort to turn to, to survive. I don't know how I'll ever be unbroken.

As I settle into my spot on the loveseat in the living room, I hear Caroline upstairs talking on the phone with her boyfriend. I worry about what it will be like for her to go back to her sophomore year of college, especially since she isn't really talking. I can tell she's angry. She needs her older brother, and he was trying to be there for her recently in a way that he couldn't always be until now. I can't seem to move, so I sit staring into the flames in the fireplace. As I do, I begin to wonder why I didn't hug my child as he headed out the door. I always did. Every time he left. I was sure I would be seeing him soon, so I called out, "I love you." That's all I did.

Oh, how I wish he was here. I wish my grandparents were here too. They would help me feel better. When I was six, I took my first airplane ride to visit Nanny and Bompa at their summer house in Maine. A cottage high above a midnight blue ocean, with wooden steps wandering down to a rocky shore, dripping with seaweed, encrusted in barnacles. Away from my dad, bathed in Nanny's loving, soft brown eyes, I found what my little girl heart dreamed there could be.

Climbing into fresh sheets, I listened to Bompa play the organ. The notes I heard, melancholy tones, struck a chord somewhere deep inside me. The crisp, salty scent of the ocean breeze coming through my window and the buoy's clinking bell lulled me to a peaceful, contented sleep. All of Maine's new sights, sounds, and smells awakened an aliveness in me.

Bompa took my brother Charlie and me to the harbor in the center of town to do some fishing. Holding each of our little palms in his own long, sun-weathered hands as we walked to the boathouse, he pointed out a lighthouse in the distance. Once we got there, Charlie and I hunched down over the water, looking below. Laying on our stomachs with our heads hanging, we spotted a starfish suctioned to the wooden posts of the dock. I inhaled the smell of freshly cut wood in the boathouse as I stepped into the back of a rowboat, tucked in next to my brother, my orange life preserver weighted around my shoulders to form a pillow.

Back on the porch at the cottage, Nanny shuffled cards by forming a bridge with her hands and letting the cards fall into place before dealing them one by one, teaching me to hold them in a fan and reminding me to make sure to keep my hand hidden. When I got restless, Nanny told me it was time to take the sea glass we'd collected, rinse off the seawater, and store it in a mason jar. She told me that the dark burgundy red and the rich royal blue pieces were the rarest finds. Dropping them into the jar, one by one, they mixed in with frosty white, turquoise, and green. Softened, Nan said, by the dancing of the waves. She set the jar on the windowsill so I could see the collage of colors glistening in the light. Could this stirring of my senses and the tenderness of my grandparents be the comforting presence Heaven offers? Is it a place where we bring each moment of love we've ever known?

The next day, the day of the funeral, I place my arms through the sleeves of the black silk blouse my sister-in-law, Perrin, and my mom found for me to wear to the service. I prepare to leave the house, calling on God for strength. I haven't been eating. I can't. I'm gone somewhere, and I'm not sure I'm coming back.

Walking into Sacred Heart Church, I picture Christopher as a shepherd, a white robe covering his head for his Christmas pageant, his first communion with a flower in his lapel, and in a suit again for his confirmation at thirteen. I walk through the side entrance to meet my family outside in the front. I steady myself as I see a group of young men gather. William, just sixteen, Chris's friend Jimmy, Chris's cousins Matthew, David, and John, and my nephew Charlie, lifting my son's coffin from the hearse. The reality of where I am and why I'm here causes my knees to buckle. I take my daughter's hand. As a big family, we fill up the whole vestibule. We are directed to stand alongside Christopher's casket as it is carried inside. The vaulted doors of the nave open, and I hold my head up high.

Awestruck by the hundreds of faces turned our direction, I begin to cry, bowing my head and putting one foot in front of the other, heading toward the altar. Once we are seated and the priest has spoken, our friends Brad and Aric begin to play a hauntingly beautiful song on their guitars written by Brad called "Prodigal Son." As I listen to the words, I think about my prodigal son and am reminded of the prodigal son role played by Brad Pitt in *A River Runs Through It*. Free-spirited, beholden to no one, gifted and cursed. No one in his family can get enough of him, yet he has his demons. In this case, in a gambling addiction that results in tragedy.

I haven't seen the movie for years, but the character is full of life and utterly captivating. You can't take your eyes off Pitt when he rebelliously dances with a lovely Native American young woman. The music conjures up that scene and kills me inside, and I slip down against the hard wood of the pew. I've heard from his friends about Chris convincing girls at the clubs that he was Brad Pitt's cousin. They bought it. I'd buy it too. Beyond the good looks, they both exude energy and charm that lights up a room. Pitt's dimples, full lips, and strong chin give me a hint of Chris's, and if I were able to smile, I would. I think about all the mothers who have raised sons they have been crazy about, tried to protect, and had to grieve. Special and flawed and glorious.

Joe, Caroline, William, and I approach the altar to read our eulogies. Joe, who understood Chris so well, strongly identified with his defiance, ADD, and passion for the Buffalo Bills, begins his reading, and his devotion to our son is potent. Caroline and William, who were given a choice not to stand up, both insisted on writing and reading their own personal tributes to their big brother. When it's my turn, I stand at the lectern and look out to the many faces and spot my mother lifting her head in my direction. This is not a gymnastics meet, a dance concert, or a delivery room, but now she will be there for me in my grief. She has lost her first grandson, which I'm not yet able to hold. I only know, as always, her presence gives me strength. I nod, stare into her soft blue eyes, then turn my eyes toward what I've written, knowing that if I look back out at the crowd, I might faint from all the emotion.

After greeting everyone and thanking them for being there, I read to them the first love letter I ever wrote to Chris. I hadn't been sure I would speak, but when I found the letter, I'd been struck by how my sentiments remained the same for his entire life. I read aloud:

I am giddy. I am simply wild about you. My feelings for you are beyond deep in a way that I am certain I share with mothers everywhere—my heart is inside out. I have an adolescent-like crush that won't fade with the passage of time. You are a sparkler in the heat of a Fourth of July night. You are my baby boy—already my one-year-old firstborn son.

    Christopher, you are a bright-eyed gift from God. So clearly you from the very start. I am not surprised by your strong presence and independence but in awe of its coexistence with your sensitivity and innocent wonder. You are strong and willful, directing all your energy outward in motion. You are an extremely active baby. There have been moments I have wished that you would lean your head on my shoulder for just a moment longer before something new caught your eye, but those moments have been treasured that much more for their brevity.

    You love being around people. You have consistently drawn people to you by reaching out and charming them as they stop to tell me how pretty your eyes are. Your family is altered by the brightness of your being. What I believed to be my capacity for love has grown beyond fullness. My prayer for you is that you experience the sheer joy you have enabled me to know.

I get through it, at one point my heart catching in my throat, but the letter perfectly captures who he was from the beginning. The only thing I might add now is that I pray Chris is able to feel the depth of my love wherever he is. This is my need, something I may have because of my father who might have told me he loved me, but I never felt it.

A firstborn myself, my mom documented my childhood in

detail. Before I could write, she transcribed my words. I must have been about six years old when she recorded my question: "How does love get inside you? I can't see it. I try to think of love, but it never comes. It never does what I want it to." I have tried to surpass my childhood wounds and ensure each of my children feels secure in my love and doesn't have to question it as I did. I want them to feel it. But now I don't have Chris here to reassure me he knew how loved he was. How loved he is and always will be.

After giving my eulogy, I return to my seat to watch Caroline and William honor their brother. I feel my sister-in-law Carolyn's hand on my shoulder as I let my tears fall. Chris's sister and brother worshipped the ground he walked on. I have never been so proud of them. They are true to themselves, Will sharing with humor and Caroline with strength. I witness such courage in my kids as they open their hearts before a church filled with what could be a thousand people.

As we drive from the service to the burial, I sit wishing we had been at the church celebrating Chris's wedding instead. He wanted to get married and settle down and have children someday. He got such pleasure from children, drew them to him. The service flowed so perfectly that Chris's spirit had to have been there. I believe he showed up. I felt him with us. I felt his presence and that of God, too, joining us in our sadness.

When we arrive at the cemetery entrance, someone texts to let me know that after we left the church, all of Chris's fraternity brothers surrounded his casket and offered up a cheer before the pallbearers carried it back outside.

The burial is harder. It's cold. The snow on the ground seeps into my shoes. I see family and select friends collecting in silhouette, black against white. When I join them, I find myself in front of a gaping muddy hole in the ground. *I don't think I can do this.* William walks over, leans his head against my shoulder, and sobs. I hold my youngest so tightly, feeling our shared pain radiate from our bodies. This is too much. I continue to hold him to my chest as the casket is lowered into the hole. I can't bear it. Each person lovingly places flowers on top of the casket and reaches out for my hand over William's shoulder as they depart back into the warmth of their cars. There is a chill that penetrates my bones, and I know I will never be the same.

four

*I*n the weeks that follow, I take a leave of absence from my job at an outpatient addiction treatment center where I have been working for the past year and a half. Once Chris started college, I'd hit the first wave of my midlife crisis and determined that it was time to renew my social work license, having let it lapse while raising my kids. I'd been fortunate to receive a great opportunity to work with my dear friend Ina, who had always cheered me on in resuming my goal of becoming a therapist. Working with alcoholics and addicts trying to get clean and sober helped me both accumulate hours toward becoming a private practice clinician and earn my specialization in addiction, which egotistically I felt like I already had.

Without the structure of my work, after dropping Caroline back at college and Will my only child at home, my therapist Ellen encourages me to take care of myself in ways I haven't been able to before. "Sally, this is the time to give yourself permission to put yourself first."

We have been working together for less than a year and, ever the caretaker, even apparently when it comes to my own therapist, I think, *Good thing she's a good therapist because she will direct me away from feeling sorry for her because she didn't know this was what she was getting, to placing my focus on myself.*

I agree with her in theory as I look around her earthy office, with its pillows, potted plants, and incense that no longer provide solace. In practice, I'm primarily concerned about making sure my kids are okay, so I insist, "But I really need to make sure William is getting to school and that Caroline is getting the support she needs."

"Yes," Ellen patiently tells me, cross-legged, her beaded wrists laying across her knees, "but unless you put your own oxygen mask on first, you will not have the capacity to do anything for anyone."

I know she's right. Much of what I've learned in the meetings for family members I've attended since we first sent Chris away to get clean and sober nearly six years ago emphasizes this point. It makes sense to me to fuel myself so I can take better care of my children. Even if it feels like I'm being selfish, I need to think of it as a healthy selfishness, where I don't place my own needs on hold anymore.

Unfortunately, I can barely do anything for anyone anyway since I'm basically saturated with grief. Every cell of my body aches for my son. My eyes are so rarely without tears that I almost don't register they are falling anymore. From time to time I notice that I've forgotten to breathe. *Just breathe, Sally. You are going to be all right.* I tell myself this repeatedly, but I am not sure I believe it. Friends and family continue to show up to sit with me in my living room or try to get me to go out and take a walk. Every action requires more effort than I've got. When I force myself to go to self-help meetings or venture past my door, I step into a world I no longer inhabit. My friend Maureen tells me I am in a parallel universe. It feels like it.

Whenever I think about leaving the house, I experience dread. My son left the house, and now I don't want to. I forget Chris isn't here. I pick up the phone to text him something, and when reality hits, knives drive into my flesh, my heart sinks. I grapple with him not being here, trying to grasp where he is now by writing to him. He's not here the way I want him to be, but is his spirit here? Joe and I console ourselves that Christopher, in being forever twenty-one, may have been spared from any additional suffering than he already experienced in his short life. We tell ourselves that he went out on top. There is some solace in believing he was not meant to grow old, that it was his path to live life in a big, bold, beautiful way and make an exit.

From my stations on the loveseat in the living room or the couch where Chris often fell asleep in the family room, I try to emulate my therapist. How can I be kinder to myself? Gentle even. I try to talk to myself more tenderly, call forth my strongest self: *Sally, you no longer need to worry about him. If you'd been able to slow him down, he would have been miserable, felt held back. It's great he got to live it his way, all-in, full-on. Try to find some peace.*

Then there's the inevitable retort from the fighter inside me. *No! I can't accept this. I want my son back.* I'm back to the ruminations of grief, the endless yearning, the feelings I want to be able to express to my son directly but can't.

Before he left for Simon's, Chris asked me whether I thought he should go into the city or head up to the lake house. I imagined the latter being the safer bet and said something like, "Simon's sounds fun, darlin.'" My defenses were down since he'd gotten safely through New Year's Eve in the city. An easy choice since, in my mind, he would be chilling out with guys, presumably taking it easy as opposed to being out on the town. I knew from experience he'd do whatever he wanted to do no matter what I suggested. I think he was a bit disappointed there weren't going to be any girls up there, but I'd been relieved that was his choice.

The harsh voice in my head berates me: *Why didn't you make him stay home? Why didn't you tell him not to go?* Was there anything I could have done to prevent this? It was my job to keep him safe. Why couldn't I?

The next days and weeks are filled with these questions. I look for answers. I try to reassure myself that it wasn't humanly possible to save my son's life. I attribute the ever-present self-blame to the fact that my fierce maternal instinct is generally on overdrive. Or, I wonder, *Does everyone else also think I failed?* It's no secret that mothers have been tasked with protecting their children from the beginning of time. I have heard other mothers say things like, "As a mom, you look at your kids and all you want to do is protect them, that's it." It's true. Since Chris died, I have also heard things like, "Well, I couldn't be too bad a mother. My kids are alive," from moms who did something like forget to make their kids dinner. Am I to conclude that I'm a bad mother? That is certainly the implication.

Nobody prepares you as a grieving parent for all the things you can expect to hear that will tear at your soul, and it factors into my not wanting to leave the house. I never feel prepared for how it's going to go out in the world, any more than I was prepared to lose him. I try not to personalize anything, but I am so raw and traumatized. Out at the grocery store one day, I overheard two moms talking. As I studied the shelves, I peered down the aisle at a short, bespectacled mom with a basket in her arms, loudly congratulating herself for letting her son go out on his own the night before. "I'm telling you, Emily, it's like I finally realized that letting him leave the house doesn't mean he's going to die." I couldn't move, remaining motionless as the conversation continued and they moved out of sight.

I don't know how to relate to people anymore. I used to be so outgoing, but now I'm anything but. I have got to develop a thicker skin and remember that people have good intentions. Already, acquaintances have made some faux pas in their attempts to connect. Expressions like, "I can't imagine," "That must be so awful," or "That's every mother's worst nightmare," feel dismissive, like they are stating the obvious, and it is the fastest way to make me feel more alone. It's hardest when there is an underlying emphasis on "I pity you." I get it. The death of a child makes people feel so powerless and afraid that they are just trying to make sense of a reality too tough to digest. However, I'd rather they acknowledge my loss with an "I'm so sorry" or a hug. If they could witness my pain without trying to fix it or even if they *could* try to imagine, it might make me feel better. Right now, it doesn't feel like too much to ask. If I can endure it, you can imagine it.

Consumed with grief, looking like the walking wounded, my loss is written all over my body. Yesterday I was notified by a florist that some flower arrangements had been dropped off for us at a house down the street. After answering my knock, I thank the young father for holding our flowers for us. He returns to the door to hand me several boxes of fresh blooms. He doesn't say a word. Usually friendly, he can't look at me and is anxious to shut the door behind him. I race back home. Of course he must know what happened. Unless he missed the news truck out front or the flocks of people coming and going.

When I was a child, we didn't have words to describe my dad's explosive behavior. Since his alcoholism wasn't recognized or named, it left room for me to make up my own story. I was left to conclude that something was very wrong and assumed it was wrong with *me*. I'm surprised when Joe tells me he thinks it's great if people avoid addressing it. For me, it feels like another "elephant in the room." I don't want to leave these interactions feeling worse, but I very much appreciate any effort to be with me in my grief, even when they don't know what to say. When friends can tolerate my pain and walk with me in it, it is the most loving thing they can do.

For me, every social interaction is awkward. The simple question, "How *are* you?" is suddenly complicated. I brace myself and overanalyze how to answer. Do they really want to know, or are they just being polite? Such a dilemma. I can reply with my standard pleasantry, "Hanging in there. How 'bout you?" or make an effort to answer truthfully. Do I try to shock them into the depths of my experience like I used to try to shock my happy-go-lucky mom? What would they do if I were to tell them the truth: "After losing my son, I often want to die."

Despite my pain and the loneliness of it during these early days spent at home, I experience an unexpected wash of grace. Held up and carried, I feel the love from family and friends in the array of colored orchids and bright arrangements on display in every room, the handwritten cards expressing their shared sorrow, the thoughtful gifts, including books on grief. Each text I receive, including the simple "thinking of you," makes a difference. I can't express how much it means when people take the time to offer compassion. I feel steeped in the bitter and the sweet simultaneously, captured in Meister Ekhart's words, "Truly, it is in the darkness that one finds the light, so when we are in sorrow, then this light is nearest of all to us."

When I take hold of my necklace, I feel like Christopher is cheering me on. "You got this, Momma!" I hear his voice in my head, and it gives me strength. While the world keeps spinning, and I don't think it should, I exist in a world between two worlds. Grief is blurry, but amid it, I feel connected. Awakened by my pain, a spiritual lightning bolt of perspective has struck. All I've ever known becomes distilled into one essential truth. Love is all that matters. It is the only thing. Chris has always taught me this, and now I finally understand.

five

For these first months, I stay home close to the fire, and for the first time ever, I'm relieved it's frigid and gray outside. I spend a lot of time on social media connecting with Christopher's friends and continue scrambling to be sure I have every photo ever taken of my son, greedily trying to accumulate every bit of proof of his very much alive self. I was always forcing him to let me take a picture when I could pin him down. He only did so reluctantly, but in pictures with his friends, he is front and center. I study everything on his phone, both so thankful to have tangible evidence of his life and disturbed that he left it behind because he should not be without it. He should be here. I panic over whether it's possible I could lose the photos, so all of them get backed up, and every print gets digitized. I know I'm in a bit of a frenzy and I don't care. I'm in an all-too-familiar position of powerlessness, just trying to do something, anything, to feel like I have control.

I continue to write to Chris: *My love for you is more powerful than any love I'd known before you arrived. Is it because you are my firstborn? Is it because you are you?* His friend Claire's mom sends me a short video. I watch as Claire arrives at her surprise party. It's a summer evening and there is a brightly burning cake. Everyone is yelling, "Woohoo, Surprise!" and then I hear Chris's distinctive chuckle in the background as it catches in his throat, and I know he was excited. There is nothing better. How I lived for his laugh. It gives me such a fix and I play it again. I feel his enthusiasm—it's contagious. He loved a party. He loved Claire and was reveling in the moment.

There were moments of intense joy soaking up his warmth and enthusiasm, and then he'd be off again. In the movie *Finding Nemo,* Dory says, "I see a light." Marlin replies, "I see it too."

Dory and Marlin are hypnotized.

"It's so pretty," says Dory.

Marlin says, "I'm feeling happy, which is a big deal for me."

Before too long a terrifying fish looms into view. Marlin says, "Good feeling's gone."

Yup, it was like that. Chris's presence filled up a room, like a balm for me, but then he'd slip through my fingers. He was my drug. If he was happy, I was too. I would do anything to see him smile. I couldn't get enough of that good feeling and was left wanting more. From the beginning, he gravitated toward friends, toward the outside world. His friends meant everything to him, and that never changed.

On Chris's first day of preschool, as other parents hugged their children and said goodbye, I stood watching him closely, his long lashes peeking out from under the unruly stick-straight pieces of hair he refused to let me cut. I was certain he would cry, as we were rarely apart. My feet were stuck to the ground. One of the teachers looked my way as she whispered to another teacher, "It can be hard for first-time moms to let go."

My pride took hold. *What's wrong with that? Wouldn't you rather have me stay so he doesn't get upset?* I was in quicksand and couldn't move. Mrs. Millner gently placed her hand on my back to shoo me out the door. I humbly walked out but hovered at the window, looking in at his sweet face, wide-eyed and not sure what to do next.

Once Chris discovered friends, he was off. To play with other little boys was his daily bread. He couldn't keep his arms from around their shoulders. At pickup, I let him run on the lawn with other little boys. Trying to get him into the car was like wrangling a puppy. He didn't want to leave them any more than I had wanted to leave him. At less than three years old, if his friends were by his side, he was completely content.

On February 27, eight weeks after losing him, Christopher's fraternity brothers invite our family to his fraternity at Northern Illinois University for a formal ceremony to celebrate his life. I don't ask Caroline and William to join us. Caroline is keeping herself very busy with school so she doesn't have to feel our sadness or her own. Since William is stuck home with us, where we are consumed with grief, I respect his interest as well in keeping his pain at arm's length. I'm conscious of letting everyone do what they need to do right now. Thankfully, Joe never hesitates to show up, so I push through my social anxiety and reluctance, knowing I'll be glad I did.

Joe and I drive to Dekalb. Joe and Caroline have already been here once to collect Chris's things and his jeep. I didn't ask them about what that had been like. I couldn't. The last time I'd been there, I had picked Chris up outside. He was sick and had scraped up his jeep and cracked the windshield. He'd not wanted us to know about it, which was why he'd called me to pick him up, but I didn't put it together until later.

Just as we walk into the fraternity house, Chris's friends Mish and Maggie arrive. We three are the only women in a room full of men. Chris shared with me about trying to impress Maggie and take her out on a nice date, but he hadn't gotten very far. He told me she wasn't ready to be in a relationship, or maybe just not with him. When I responded with surprise, he admitted that his drunken behavior wasn't always so endearing.

I feel self-conscious as the ceremony gets underway. I'm wearing Chris's blue and yellow Buffalo jersey, not having taken into consideration that the boys would be dressed in sportscoats and ties. Chris's fraternity brothers are taking the service very seriously, adhering to their house guidelines as they perform each step. The room becomes quiet, the curtains are drawn, and the light is dim. It's so strange to be standing with all his brothers in this house where Chris spent all his time for the past few years and not have him appear from around the corner.

The ceremony concludes after one of the boys hands me a single white rose. Then Joe and I follow a bunch of the guys down the stairs to their basement party room. I smell the pungent, strangely comforting scent of beer emanating from the floor and picture my child here, the life of the party. In the pool room off to the side, Sam and Alyx show up to join Mish, Maggie, and me. Joe heads over to the bar with the guys. Mish begins to tear up as the girls tell me how Chris spent a lot of time in this room. I cry, too, but I am used to it by now. Rarely are my cheeks dry, but in front of other people I have mastered the art of crying quietly.

Being here with Chris's friends I have a sensation of what it might feel like to have a celebrity son. The girls giggle when I say this out loud.

"In his own way, he was famous, Mrs. McQ," Sam says.

Mish is graduating this year, so I hand her a gift to celebrate her accomplishment. It's a set of two sterling silver bracelets with one of Christopher's tweets on it. I'd gotten my own rendition of this gift from my coworker Gaby and was so touched by it that I have been ordering more for family and friends. She inscribed the bracelets with his words, "Life is honestly so beautiful as long as you allow it to be."

When I first studied my son's words, I was awed by his

wisdom. Each morning when I put my bracelets on, I take Christopher's message to heart. I encourage myself to reach beyond feeling sorry for myself because I can no longer lay my eyes on his beauty and instead allow life to be beautiful by focusing on the beauty of his spirit. If I can "rejoice because thorn bushes have roses" instead of "complaining that rose bushes have thorns," I am making a conscious choice to place my attention on the love he gave and trying to spread it.

Mish places the bracelets on her wrist as I tell her I don't know what Chris would have done without her once she'd graduated and that I hope his words give her comfort. She takes my arm and pulls me aside, "Chris was an angel sent from heaven to me. He was the younger brother I never had. We got to have the kind of friendship every guy and girl should have in this lifetime. It's not easy to talk about, but I just want you to know, Mrs. McQ. He always called me the 'angel of his world.'"

I get the chills because that's what *I* called him. "I have so many terms of endearment I use for those I adore, but I only ever used that one for him." As I tell her this, it dawns on me that Mish must have cared for him like I would, and I'm so grateful.

She looks so sad, so I hold her close and reassure her, "I know if he called you that, you were extra special to him." I look into her brown eyes and place my hand on her shoulder. "I get the sense you probably did some taking care of him along the way."

She smiles, nods her head, and tells me about how he roped her into doing more than a little bit of his laundry. A smile begins to form on my lips as we rejoin the girls who are looking up at a huge glass shadow box on the wall. It's a tribute to Chris, with one of his Hawaiian shirts hung in the center. Maggie put it together. I can tell she *did* care about him when she quietly says, "Chris put everyone before himself. All he ever wanted was for others to be happy."

Before we join up with the guys, another friend shows me the brass plaque they made in Chris's honor which reads, "Live Life Lavishly," in bold letters. I can definitely see him saying that, endorsing living life in the moment, not ostentatiously, but all-in. Alyx, who reminds me of a little pixie, keeps rubbing my shoulder, and I begin to absorb how his friends have loved him. I soak up their love and give it right back. And they let me.

Then we girls meet up with the guys at the party room bar, where Joe shows me the framed Buffalo Bills Jersey that each of the boys has signed. Joe tells me they presented it to him, chipping in together for a fresh jersey instead of Chris's well-worn one, with the same number and the McQuillen name on the back. Being a huge Bills fan himself, like his dad, Chris had converted his fraternity brothers into fans as well. Joe, who I'd only seen cry a few times before Chris died, is loudly sobbing.

I find out Chris had a fraternity dad and a fraternity son. His "dad" Nick approaches me, reminding me that he and Chris went to St. John together. He tells me how they immediately recognized each other from when they played football together. I tell him he's the reason Chris chose AKL instead of the other fraternity that was recruiting him. He smiles, something about him reminding me of my son. He shares with me how one day, in the middle of a long winter, Chris turned to him and said, "Dude, let's drop everything and move to Key West."

"How will we afford it?" Nick asked.

"We will get jobs at bars or restaurants because we are both such good-looking, outgoing guys," Chris replied.

Nick tells me about what a natural leader Chris was and how he studied hard to become a member of AKL. I interrupt and tell him I think Chris studied harder for the fraternity than he did for school. Then he introduces me to Surry, Chris's "son," and I want to cry. These boys all look like they could be related. Looking into their eyes, I feel their affection for my boy, and instantly, they have my heart.

I ask if we can see Chris's room, which I know now sits empty. As we walk up the stairs, I imagine my son racing up alongside us, and I find that I'm getting excited—Christopher excited— the excitement I always felt whenever he was around or about to be. I haven't felt anything that compares to the way I felt when I saw his jeep pulling into the driveway. I want to taste that feeling of having him close again.

When we enter his room, there's an electric charge in the air. We all crowd into his old room, facing where his bed was. I don't know how, but I feel his energy all around me. His friends are hushed. My heart is both heavy and light. I try to joke with his roommate, Raul, that Chris was probably a messy roommate. I look at him, but at first, he can't return my gaze. I can't think about what this must have been like for him, especially since he had to move out of their shared room after the accident. He lifts his head and tries to smile my way. "We took care of each other, Mrs. McQ. He made my life at college 1000 percent better. He's a legend." I can tell there is nothing more he can say without breaking down.

I don't want to leave. It feels like he's here. Here in this room, with his fraternity brothers and girlfriends, it is abundantly clear that he spent this chapter of his life surrounded by affection. I spot a bright-blonde girl with big brown eyes and recognize her from lots of pictures where she is by my son's side. It turns out Chris and Gina were close. She tells me he looked out for her like a big brother, and I give her a hug. I stand there experiencing their love for him and feel the warmth of it. Flooded with gratitude, I realize there was never any need to worry about him here.

I only wish my concern about his drinking hadn't caused him to keep this life as separate from me as he had. I'd understood that wanting to be like everyone else meant he would resume drinking after three years of sobriety. I never wanted him to feel ashamed or different, but my concern was hard to hide. Now, I get it. College and drinking couldn't exist, one without the other, and he wouldn't have wanted to forego this love and brotherhood once he had it.

*C*rying in the car on the drive home from Dekalb, I think about how last spring, after a year-and-a-half in college, things had started to catch up to Chris. He'd called to tell me he wanted to come home from school for a night. Joe and I jumped at the chance to meet him and take him out for a nice dinner, but the moment I laid eyes on him, I could tell something was wrong. I joined him at the bar as Joe parked the car after dropping me off. I watched Chris quickly polish off a few beers. I knew from the way he threw them back that he wasn't going to be able to outrun his alcoholism. Even though we'd caught it early and he'd been sober three years from age sixteen to nineteen, he hadn't been able to apply all his learning about addiction to make his disease go away as he'd hoped he could.

Of course I'd already known that self-knowledge doesn't cure us from alcoholism, but as his mom, I had prayed maybe I was wrong. I should have known. He'd come home a month earlier with bruises from falling at school in a blackout. I'd seen something he'd posted on Facebook recently too—a long list of numbers followed by empty spaces titled, "This is a list of all the girls that like me."

I'd mentioned it to him. "My love, you have no idea. I know there are so many young women who have crushes on you even if

Maggie didn't work out." I was accustomed to watching women hit on him. In fact, it happened every time we were out together.

He'd turned to me, placed his hand on my shoulder, and abruptly stated, "Yeah, but when I forget that I talked to them the night before, the charm pretty much wears off." I knew what that shame felt like, and I steeled myself against that pain, always experiencing his so vicariously.

At dinner that night, Chris was mostly quiet, but he let us know that the wheels were starting to come off and he was failing his classes. I could tell how hard it was for him to admit this. His struggles with school had been an ongoing cross for him to bear, and I didn't want to make him feel worse. School was challenging enough for him without the alcohol, and if his drinking was worsening, there was no way he'd be able to pull it off. Not knowing what else to do, he agreed to try to get sober again. Joe was gung-ho about hooking him up with a monthly refresher program. So, Chris finished up his spring semester and then agreed to spend time that summer in a short-term residential treatment. He didn't even tell his friends where he was going.

That June, while in treatment, the rest of us joined my brothers and their families in Colorado at a YMCA ranch family reunion. I was miserable because I wanted Chris to be with us. I wasn't convinced he was ready to resume a sober lifestyle, however, especially since he'd have to leave college to do it. While my family members enjoyed the zipline, I sat at an outdoor chapel facing a large wooden cross at the base of the mountains, praying that he could find his way back. I knew his partying could lead to further suffering, and I didn't want that for him.

By the end of July, Joe had gotten Chris settled into a sober living apartment in Minnesota where I hoped he would meet lots of young sober people, stay there, and settle into a new life putting his sobriety first. Joe returned home confident that things were good. I wanted to believe him but couldn't share in his optimism. I could see it in pictures Joe took of their time together: Chris wasn't happy. When the rest of us came together for the McQuillen family reunion in Canada in early August, I wondered again whether this was a missed opportunity to be with him if this plan didn't take. Thus began my endless phone calls from Canada, trying to encourage him to hang in there.

The calls all played out the same way: "Mom, this isn't so great. I'm stuck here with a bunch of older guys and nothing to do."

"What about all the young people that Dad said were out there? That is why you're there, sweetie, so that you can meet people your age who are going to meetings and living sober too. Have you connected with any young people? Dad said something about a softball league."

"Nahhh, not really. Just the old guys here at the apartment. Not much happening."

"You sound down, babe. Can you hang in there a bit? Give it some time?"

But he had made up his mind. I hated to think about how he had invested in a fresh start and was throwing it away. I knew he was depressed, and I felt so powerless and far away. There was no convincing him to stick it out, especially since I didn't realize the power of the brotherhood he had left behind at AKL. He found out he could take classes nearby at a community college in Dekalb and continue to live in his fraternity house. That was all it took. He immediately packed up and left Minnesota, hightailing it back to school and to his friends.

Something inside me shifted after that. I was still desperate to ensure my son was safe, but I also knew there was nothing I could do. I had to let go. I went to self-help meetings and worked hard in therapy sessions to release my fear. I trusted that God was looking out for him as I could not. I threw myself into my work at the treatment center and focused on becoming detached enough to let him live his own life and not let my fear interfere with our relationship. He was twenty-one, no longer the sixteen-year-old whose life we tried to save by sending him away for help. It was time to trust that he would make his way back to sobriety in his own time.

Back to school that fall, he wasn't particularly communicative. He probably felt as if he'd disappointed us, but that wasn't the case. My sole focus was on letting him know how unconditionally loved and accepted he was by being free of an agenda or my worry when calling, texting, and leaving him messages. I tried, as always, to respect his need for space and independence. I could tell he was back to being fully engaged in his life at school. When he did call me back, he appreciated all the affection coming his way, and an ease resumed in our relationship.

A week after the AKL Memorial, my brother Rick invites me to California so I can join him, my sister-in-law, Perrin, and their two-year-old Emma for a few days during their month-long stay to break up the Chicago winter. It's been six weeks, and everyone is encouraging me to get some sunshine and enjoy time with Emma. Joe tells me he can hold the fort down with William. Typically, I'd see Rick's offer as a dream come true—I love to travel, and I've never been to La Jolla—but the idea of leaving home at all fills me with unease, and I feel conflicted. I haven't felt any enthusiasm these past few months. The thrill is gone. I see other people smiling and wonder what that would be like. It will take much more energy than I've got to get there, but I decide it will be good for me. I tell myself nothing is more important than being with people you cherish.

I am a big sister to three younger brothers, Charlie, Rick, and Douglas, and a big half-sister by twenty years to my dad's other kids, Christina and Nicholas. I'm stepsister to my stepdad's sons, Greg and Steve, and their wives, Kimberly and Wendy. Doug flew in from Texas and Christina from Oregon for Chris's funeral, which meant the world to me since I don't get to see them very often. Greg and Kimberly flew in from Colorado. Nicholas lives in France, and we rarely get to see each other. Despite Charlie and Rick living in the same state as me, I don't see either of them enough. When Rick and his first wife divorced, an already close connection between us deepened. He is five years younger than I am, so when he met Perrin and they got pregnant with Emma, my kids were already in their adolescence. It felt like the closest thing to getting to have another child of my own. Even before Emma arrived, I was certain she would be exactly who she is—sweet as cherry pie with an extra squeeze of orange zest mixed in.

When I get down on the floor to play with her, she spins in circles, arms outstretched. I tell her not to get too dizzy, and she plops onto the floor, smiling. Rolling around in her flowered dress, she giggles as I tickle her. She takes away some of my devastation. Her playful blue eyes catch the light, and her auburn curls bounce, melting away the frost beginning to form around my heart. It's like her little soul can see mine, like she is telling me to keep my heart open. Only two, she is smart, has lots to say, and somehow understands that her cousin is in Heaven. When I mention Chris's name, she looks up at me and, in her little voice, says, "Awwwwww, Sal," and I am crazy about her for it. She sees me. When I can be in the present moment with Emma, I feel okay. Chris got such a kick out of her and posted a profile picture on Instagram of him holding her on his lap.

He also tweeted, "Little cousin just told me she wanted me to get her a flying unicorn for Christmas. Fuck man idk if I'm going to be able to deliver." The tone of this one-liner brings him and his humor to life.

After playing with Emma, I walk down past blocks of houses toward the ocean. I approach an opening filled with large craggy rocks, surprised that no one else is here. I climb onto one of the highest rocks and sit watching the waves crash and break into spray below. I fall into a trance as I study the vastness of the sea as the tide rolls in. There is something so reassuring about the motion of the tide's ebb and flow. No matter how my world has been altered, the forces of nature keep doing what they do. The sun descends closer to the horizon. The seagulls fly overhead and perch beneath me on a mossy ledge. I am calmed by my smallness and the sounds of nature swirling all around me.

Back home from a week in California, our neighborhood is doused in gray. The snow has delicately descended upon the trees, but I can't appreciate its beauty. The damp seeps into the old floorboards of our home. Even my heavily socked toes feel cold.

Where are you?

I stare out the window and wonder whether life on earth is only one of many lives and if there are many more to follow. If I could wrap my brain around the possibility that our soul lives on and on, maybe death would feel less frightening, abrupt, and final than it does. My grief is like the ocean, throwing me against rocks, chipping shards of pain from my heart and casting them out to sea. And when the next wave arrives, I'm gutted. My sadness weighs me down, hangs heavy. I am breathing but I can't get air in my lungs. I overthink, revisit decisions, and pull myself inside out with a guilt I can't flesh out.

The questions percolate. Did I give him too much space? Not enough? I'm a broken record in my head, questioning every decision I ever made as Chris's mom. How many times have I heard someone say that their parents did the "best they could?" It sounds like they are making excuses for the ways their parents failed them. I have never been able to go easy on myself when it comes to my parenting. And now the guilt is overwhelming. I have concluded that I failed. I couldn't protect him. I couldn't save him. That is a mother's job, and I came up short. Even when I tried as hard as I could to not be afraid of what might happen when Christopher returned to school, I'm sure he could feel the unease I tried to hide. I bet he felt my fear from the beginning.

Being newly returned from the California sunshine and bracing back against the bitterness of a midwestern winter, I schedule a massage. I decide that this is no longer an indulgence but a necessity in the throes of grief. Face down under a white sheet, Angelica digs her fingers into the knotted connection between muscle and bone behind my shoulder blade. She lands on a deeper layer of muscle that feels tightly braided and needs release. At first, I squeeze my eyes shut tight, wanting to scream from the physical pain. Then I allow my breath to escape. Relief results from entering the pain, not guarding against it. As in all things, I need to let go. I need to lean into my emotional pain without fighting it. Like going on a "bear hunt," I can't go over or under it, but I can be in it and still be okay. As my breath deepens, I unclench my teeth and my jaw relaxes. With each pass of Angelica's hands, she kneads the stress from my body.

On the drive home, I turn up the volume of my music, struck by how, in one song after another, someone is pining after someone who's gone. There are a few spots on the ground where the snow has begun to puddle into miniature ponds, but winter is far from over. In the yards I pass, I spot little islands where the green reveals itself under the snow, and a rare ray of sunshine enters my car window.

Approaching the sanctuary of our cozy home with its forest green shutters, I picture Joe and I standing at the front step for the first time with baby Christopher. It was the second house we looked at in the suburbs, my grandparents at our side. My grandmother, Nanny, pointed out that if we bought it, we'd be living across the street from where they first settled. Joe immediately fell in love with it. So did I. We have been here ever since.

I pull past our slate walk, wondering when spring will arrive, and dreamily return to an April morning nearly twenty-two years earlier when Christopher was about to be born. There was a promise in the air as spring buds peeked out from the earth. I pushed my firstborn into the world in ten excruciating minutes in the middle of Tax Day. His fast-paced delivery catapulted me into my new life as a mother. Elatedly looking into his sparkly eyes for the first time, I felt awash in a love that was exhilarating, breathtaking, and profound.

Christopher was a colicky baby. His discomfort was intolerable to me from the start. If he wasn't content, I couldn't be. In his first years of life and my first time as a mother, Chris quickly became everything to me, an answer to a longing I didn't know I'd had. When he wasn't in seeming distress during his first three months, there was an innocence and sweetness to him that mirrored a long-lost part of myself. Colors deepened, the sky brightened, and he became my why.

Crawling out of his crib and running by nine months meant

Chris was off to the races before I was ready to let him go. His pacifier was the only steadfast reminder that he was still a baby since he was always on the move and never looked back. I didn't realize it then, but from the start, alongside my overpowering affection for my boy, there was an accompanying fear that something so precious to me could be taken away.

Ever since Chris went back to school after his stint at treatment that summer, the fear that always lurked beneath the surface had started to truly lift for the first time I could ever remember. I was hoping he could do well enough in community college to return to NIU, where he wanted to become a special education teacher. The despair I initially felt when he went back to a life of drinking led to more letting go. I prayed the "Child of Light" prayer for him each morning, attended my self-help meetings and therapy sessions, intent on releasing my fear, and concentrated on the only thing I had control over, which was just to love him.

And then, as if it were some sort of sick joke, I lost him. What am I to conclude from this? That my fear could have saved him? That I had been wrong to release my fears only to have my greatest fear realized? That I shouldn't have had faith in God after all? I know in my heart that isn't true. I don't think God was punishing me, nor do I think that God would have rewarded me by making sure he survived. As if God favors those parents whose children live longer. I believe God has a plan and that free will plays a powerful role in the outcome.

I know I need to stop agonizing over whether I should have done anything differently. I question my actions as if I ever possessed the power to keep him here. I don't even know if God could. Being at the whim of grief's pull feels overwhelming and confusing and impossible to handle gracefully. I want to be able to someday hold my head up, let go of the guilt, and come to peace that I really did do the very best I could.

seven

*I*n March, my friend Janet encourages me to meet with a medium she describes as the "real deal" and arranges for it to happen. Since I appreciate more than ever that life is short, I seize the chance to participate in an upcoming small group reading in Denver. Admittedly, I'm desperate to connect with my son. The possibility that I can communicate with him in some way is incredibly alluring. At the same time, I'm skeptical. What if I fly there for this and Chris doesn't even come through? I'm not sure I can face that kind of disappointment right now. *Chris, should I go for it?* I decide it's worth the risk. I'll do anything that brings me closer to my child, anything to gain a sense that my son is "still here."

The next morning, after arriving at my destination early, I'm directed to find a seat in a large office space designed for group readings. I pick a spot on the edge of a long, creamy crouch facing a coffee table with a huge quartz crystal rising from its center. I lean back against a woven pillow, cross my legs in front of my chest, and hug myself tight as the other group members wander into the room. We acknowledge each other, but I don't tell them anything about myself. A few of them introduce themselves and tell me I will love Rebecca, as they have met with her before. I don't volunteer much. Without totally realizing I'm doing it, I'm making sure this is for real. I need proof that it is truly possible to connect to my son.

When Rebecca Rosen walks into the room minutes later, pregnant and petite, her slim wrists encircled with mala beads, the anxious energy in the room lifts. We listen closely as she educates us about how the session will go. She sits in front of a large golden Buddha facing the group. There are eight of us, and I've only met the ones seated closest to me—an older couple and a young man who walked in and sat next to me on the couch. I have no idea who they have lost and are hoping to hear from.

"Heaven is what we want it to be. What we make it. I will try to channel each of your loved ones, but please understand that if they don't come through directly, messages from other people's loved ones are likely intended for you as well." She goes on to tell us that those who have "crossed over" maintain their personalities in spirit, so if they are shy, they could possibly hold back, while other spirits step forward. I exhale, knowing that if Chris is out there, his strong personality will make itself known. She leads us in a meditation after explaining that spirits are made up of energy and that she needs to raise her vibration to connect.

I pull the charcoal gray alpaca scarf Chris brought me from Peru out of my bag and tuck it in my lap. Joe insists that having something with Chris's energy on it will help him come through. When the meditation is done, Rebecca immediately turns to a man across from me, asking him whether he's on the edge of something scientific. He states, "I'm a doctor." His wife, seated by his side, chimes in that he is using new surgical techniques in his practice.

"It's your uncle. He wants you to know that this is your life's purpose and that you will be helping more people than you can imagine." Rebecca smiles as she relates this.

After the man humbly thanks his uncle for coming through, Rebecca turns to me, brushing her long, wavy hair from her face.

"You are a healer too. I see a green glowing light around you."

I freeze. All I can do is nod. Before I can tell her about being a therapist, she turns back to the man's wife and begins to channel additional messages for her. I'm spellbound, listening closely, as I can see this happens quickly, and Rebecca appears to be at the whim of the spirits just as much as we are.

"Does anyone know a Jerry?" she asks. I wait to see if any of the other people present say that they do. I'm sure it can't be my brother-in-law.

"Someone here has to know a Jerry," she utters with some urgency.

I squeak out, "It could be my husband's brother?"

"Jerry is excited," she says. "Jerry, please wait until I finish here." She attempts to connect for the doctor's wife again, telling her that her mother wishes her a happy birthday. Slightly flustered, Rebecca stops and turns back to me. "I'm sorry. Jerry is being very impatient. Let's just see what he has to say."

I can't believe it. If this is Jerry, he would absolutely be persistent and impatient, just like my husband. Talk about personalities remaining consistent. Joe's older brother Jerry passed away from cancer just a few years ago. Jerry was like a father figure to Joe as one of the oldest of ten children, and I adored him.

"He is okay," Rebecca tells me. "He is so happy to let you know he is with a Robert."

I can't believe it. "That's Bobby, his brother." I'm reeling. Bobby took his life when Joe was in college, and he rarely talks about him.

"Yes, Jerry is with Bobby. Jerry is telling me he is like the patriarch of his family."

"Ten kids," I say louder than I mean to. "He was the oldest boy of ten siblings." I wonder if this is what he was trying to tell her.

I'm stunned, attempting to wrap my head around all of this. She is somehow interpreting what these spirits communicate and then feeling it out with us. This is like nothing I've ever experienced before. I'm pleased to hear from Jerry, but I'm preoccupied with wanting to hear from Christopher. I'm doing all that I can to stay present, and yet, I'm not able to entirely process what is happening. I dig my fingers into my scarf and try to stay focused.

Rebecca returns to channeling the doctor's wife's mother. She asks the woman if she knows a Mary, and someone else on the other side of the room says, "No, but I know a Marie." And so it goes for a while, a bit mind-boggling to follow the ping-pong of messages she's trying to receive and deliver.

Rebecca turns her attention to a young woman on my left who hasn't stopped crying. I don't want to cry, so I listen intently, looking away from her tear-stained face. Rebecca tells her that her husband wants to reassure her he knows she'll be able to take care of their young children without him. The young woman begins to tell us how she'd recently had to identify her husband's body after his car was crushed by a truck. I feel how traumatized she is. I become squeamish as she describes the blood. She crumples tissues in her hands as Rebecca asks, "What can you tell me about a ladybug?"

She reaches down to the hem of her jeans and lifts it up so we can see that there is a little red spotted ladybug tattooed on her ankle. "I got this in honor of my two-year-old son."

Oh my God. This is too much. She lost her baby too.

My breathing slows as Rebecca reassures her, "You were not intended to save his life. Your son was an old soul meant to be on this earth for only a short time. Drowning is one of the most peaceful ways to go."

Were those words meant for me? My breathing picks up again.

I'm moving into an altered state even as I hang onto every word. My head no longer feels connected to my body.

Right then, Rebecca stops and asks all of us, "Who is the alcoholic?"

I wait for someone else in the room to answer. No one does. The room feels too quiet, and I feel a chill as I hear myself say, "My son."

She nods at the young mother and at me, explaining that spirits will bring forward other spirits. "Ohhhh, now I understand," she says as if all of this is a matter of fact. "He is coming in on the heels of her son because he also drowned."

Facing me directly now, she says, "Your son is an old soul too." Again, the room is quiet. It's true. She's right. I start to drift away and then pull myself back to earth. I try to catch the young woman's eye to acknowledge our common loss, but she has slunk down into her chair and doesn't look up.

Rebecca looks me in the eye and says, "Your son assumes responsibility for making a poor choice that led to his death. This was not an intentional death. It was an accident. He is okay."

I already know it was an accident, but her validation that he's okay is so necessary. I desperately need to know that my child didn't suffer and wasn't afraid. Rebecca continues, "He is telling me that there is some irony in the timing of his death."

I think about it, "Yes. He died on January 3, after making it through a crazy New Year's Eve."

"Was there drinking and driving involved in his death?"

"There was drinking. He and some friends were partying and decided to take a canoe out on a frozen lake. None of them survived." I will not use the word drowned. I feel like I'm about to leave my body entirely.

"He is sorry," Rebecca tells me. "He is also grateful that you have forgiven the situation."

I take that in and know that it's true. I have forgiven it. I don't blame anyone. I don't blame him. I don't blame the alcohol and drugs. This could have happened to any young adult under the influence. I would never blame Chris for being his adventurous self.

Just as I am letting this begin to absorb, I hear, "Why am I seeing Reese's peanut butter cups?" "Oh my God. They were his favorite candy. I always sent them to him in care packages." I'm truly surprised. I feel excited as if he's right here. *Is he?* She thanks him for stopping by as if she wishes they could have more time together. *Who wouldn't? Again, it fits.* I'm in a daze as she proceeds to channel other spirits.

All I can do is shake my head and sit, watching more of these magical exchanges take place for the other people in the room. At the end of the session, Rebecca asks us whether we have questions for her. I picture Chris laughing at me as I pull out my list.

I swallow, then pose my first question. "Is it possible that my fear my son would die could have caused it to happen?" Until I wrote this question out the night before, I hadn't even consciously realized it had been plaguing me.

Immediately she replies, "Definitely not. The intuition you had about it on a soul level was designed to prepare you for his early departure." I experience a flicker of relief that can't yet land and greedily ask, "Was my son afraid when he died? Did he suffer?"

She asks, "Christopher, were you afraid?"

I wait for what feels like an eternity, tears now prickling at my eyes, and she says, "He left right away without suffering."

I'm breathing in staccato as I ask, "Will I see him again?"

"Yes, he will be there to greet you. You are a magnet for him.

He loves you asking for him. He is kind of like an angel for you."

This last thing she says soothes my heart. It validates that this message comes from him. Chris has always been my angel. It is the word Chris would choose, and she has given it voice. After the session is over, I say my goodbyes, feeling a touch of buoyancy and some hesitancy as well, in case I'm just being gullible.

Back home from Denver, the gift of connecting with Chris begins to sink in as I share it with Joe. My doubts about a medium's ability to connect with souls on the other side have subsided. Plus, I got a Christopher fix. But then, there is a letdown. Like a hangover. Getting to bask in his glow this way wasn't enough. Now I feel guilty for wanting more. Joe has experienced this kind of letdown after a reading, too, and we agree it's a consequence of getting to have a moment of connection followed by more letting go.

Here again, gone again, the glow has dimmed. It doesn't help when I pull myself together enough to attend a book group with friends that night and risk telling them about my experience only to have it fall flat. A few of them try to give me the benefit of the doubt, try to listen respectfully, but I feel their disbelief. The one friend I thought was most likely to take satisfaction from my experience looks at me like I've lost my mind. She tries to get my attention over the tops of other women's heads as she pours herself a glass of wine. "You don't really believe Chris actually showed up, do you?" I pretend I haven't heard her when another friend joins us and provides a distraction. I end up with my tail between my legs, back to doubting and feeling alone.

The next day, sorting through some of Chris's things, I take another hit. I feel guilty to begin with because I've opened a notebook and discovered a bucket list Chris must have written when he was in Minneapolis last summer. I am not the kind of mom to read her children's diaries. I have trespassed. I begin to feel dizzy, but I can't turn away. It includes things like:

* Learn to sail.
* Learn to play guitar.
* Meet Jimmy Buffet.
* Go to a Buffalo Bills Superbowl.
* Become a father.
* Provide for my parents when they are too old.
* Attain absolute contentedness.

God damn-it! I can't do this. I can't live without him. I am gutted. I want to call out to Chris and have him reassure me that he's okay. This list brings his presence close, but it also brings unremitting pain. He didn't get to do these things. I listen for him but can't hear his voice. Just a faint *you got this, Momma.* I try to replicate his stutter in my head, conjure up the times his thoughts would collect more quickly than he could express them. How I'd have to ask him to repeat himself. Could it be possible that he can be here with me and be wherever he is? Since I have decided Heaven has to exist if that's where my child is, I begin to shift from thinking about it as an abstraction into a definitive place. It helps me to try to form a picture of Chris in a state of awe and bliss. It's like I'm looking through a kaleidoscope, waiting for the colors to crystallize. I've read that spirits can be in more than one place at a time, so maybe he's busy helping other spirits in Heaven and hanging out to help all the people who are still here missing him like crazy.

If Heaven is what we want it to be, I envision Chris as he looked in a picture taken on his trip to Machu Picchu, sitting on the side of a mountain surrounded by orphan children leaning against his shoulders—his baseball cap tilted back and his face lit up by the sun. I want him to be filled with joy, without the sorrow I know existed beneath the surface. This was the place where he and I were most alike, in the deeply feeling place that fosters empathy and a desire to relieve the suffering of those we love. Our sensitivity intensifying our experience could sometimes make it feel like too much. This is why I like to imagine Heaven as a soothing deep blue sky where Christopher plays with children and animals and feels the limitless love of God, family, and friends all around him.

I recognize that I begin to bargain as I grieve his future. What if his life had gotten worse? He died when life was good and the consequences of his drinking hadn't brought him completely to his knees. This would mean he was spared more pain. If an afterlife exists, I want to think he is being cared for beyond my imagining. If I can only allow myself to believe he didn't suffer, as Rebecca said he did not, and has attained the contentedness he sought, I can find some peace.

eight

*W*hen I spot the tiniest fresh buds on the tips of our forsythia bushes, I know spring has arrived. Typically, sunlight breaking through the monotony of a white sky, early shoots of green emerging from the dirt, and the return of birdsong after our long winters bring a lift. Instead of brightness this year, my senses feel dull, as if my windows are still awash in streams of rain even after the storm has passed. The season's effects on me have flip-flopped. Even joyful memories are a source of pain. No filling up Chris's pale blue Easter basket this year, no jellybean trail, no foil-wrapped chocolate bunnies, no Reese's egg. I revisit all the ways parents celebrate our kids, and grief swallows me. Being our first, Chris set the tone, beginning with Joe's over-the-top idea to have pony rides on our front lawn for his first birthday party. The elation of those celebrations juxtaposed against the emptiness I feel today is dramatic.

Anticipating Chris's April birthday, I am mourning him both this birthday and every birthday party we ever had— Chuck E. Cheese, Power Rangers, parachutes, and paintball. It was always a production with cake, ice cream, and goodie bags. I remember his Christening Day, holding my baby in my arms as the service was performed. I'd not had any interaction with a priest before. This tall man in his white robe had such a powerful presence that I felt like a child as I stood before him. I felt humbled, as if I should be showering him with offerings of gratitude for the miracle of my son. A light shone through the stained-glass chapel window onto Chris, Joe and me, his godparents, grandparents, and great-grandparents, all of us beaming as he was baptized.

After the service, we marched to the melody of the bagpipers who followed us from the church to our friend's home for a reception. Christopher, only three months old, acted as if he already knew we would gather around him adoringly for the rest of his life. We formed a spring parade, taking us past green lawns into the middle of the street. I'd at first blushed at the idea when Joe presented it. "Bagpipes? Are you serious?" But I was surprised by how right it felt. When faced with the decision about Christopher's burial, Joe again insisted on having bagpipes. Their melancholy tones played as we lay our son to rest in Sacred Heart Cemetery, but this time I barely registered the sound.

I know it's only the beginning. Grief feels, three months in, as if the blade of a knife is tearing through what is left of my heart. It hasn't just penetrated my skin. The knife stays lodged inside my wounds, digging and thrashing. Every step I take from our home to my car is made against winds that don't exist. My yearning to have my son back is so constant and strong that it almost feels powerful enough to bring him back to life. I get in my jeep and stare at his picture. His prayer card sits in the center of my dashboard, secured by a heart-shaped rock. All I can do is think about him.

Driving the fifteen minutes to the cemetery, I don't even realize that's where I'm headed. But I am consumed with constant longing, as if my body is starving, carved out with a hunger that can't be satiated. There is a gravitational pull to my son's grave. My body is made of lead, but I drag myself from my car to his gravestone, thinking about the physical effects of grief. The heaviness and exhaustion, the migraines I've never had before, with black spots and flickering lights that interrupt my vision. The doctor calls them auras and can't tell me what's causing them. I wonder if it's because I am crying more tears than I knew was humanly possible.

I sit at Chris's gravestone and rub my fingers across the letters engraved in the dark granite—his full name, birth, and death dates underneath. The sensation of gently moving my hand from side to side feels comforting as it would if I were stroking his head and brushing his hair across his cowlick. I want to die, but I hold on. I smile at the Buffalo Bills logo on his stone, water the flowers, and find it is peaceful here. This will be a spot where I can take care of him since I can no longer take care of him. Just then, a little bird flies past the top of an angel statue nearby. I wave at it and blow it a kiss as if it's my son saying "hi" and watch it fly toward the trees out of sight.

On Chris's birthday, April 15, I sit with his baby book in my lap. Paging through my detailed notes and glued pictures brings his early childhood to life. When he turned two, I wrote, "There is a spirit of forward movement about you that comes from within. It is in your nature to move freely without holding back. You are seemingly always in motion."

I think now about how my mom had broached the subject of his hyperactivity with me and how I'd bristled. She told me that even though I was her only girl, I had been her busiest child and that Christopher was far busier than I had been. I didn't have a frame of reference, and I suppose I was defensive and in some denial about the prospect of my child being in any way different.

I return to Christopher's baby book and chuckle when I appreciate, again, how much he was himself from the start. I just had to catch up. At age two, I'd written him a love letter with the intention that he'd look back on it someday. It recounted that "now" and "no way!" were some of his favorite words. Toward the end of the letter, I confessed, "Sometimes I lose patience with my not surprisingly strong-willed child, but I'm crazy about strong personalities. After all, I married your dad." Now I feel guilty for ever being impatient and for every other thing I wish I'd done better.

As he grew, Chris continued to be filled with energy, and, regrettably, my patience could wear thin. He was a complex mix of charm, busyness, and sensitivity, and by the time Caroline arrived, I found myself in bookstores, purchasing books with titles like *Your Busy Child, Your Challenging Child, Your Demanding Child.* My boy was easily overstimulated, impulsive, and never still. I attributed being challenged to not having done this parenting thing before. But there was more to it.

The first indication I had that Christopher's energy level wasn't typical was when gathering with other moms and sharing that I felt challenged by his persistence and restlessness. I asked if they felt similarly challenged, and when no one responded it became clear they couldn't relate to my overwhelmed condition. Once I had Caroline, she helped me appreciate the possibility that some children didn't constantly need to be moving. Seeing that Chris was different reminded me how much I'd hated feeling different as a child. Whether being a child of an alcoholic (ashamed of her father's behavior without understanding why) or as the first child I knew whose parents got divorced, the "different than" dye had been cast, and I wanted to spare my son from that feeling.

My father's behavior as an alcoholic was unpredictable and left me with dread as I wasn't sure what kind of a mood he'd be in when he walked in the door at night after work. His volatility and anger frightened me as a child, though I couldn't have articulated it at the time. I didn't know what I'd done to make my dad get so angry, and my only certainty was that something would inevitably set him off.

One night after dinner I had a typical little-girl meltdown and threw myself on the floor of the kitchen. "You're being dramatic," Dad said, and I knew he was going to begin a lecture. "Now you're going to stay there. You can't get up until I tell you to. Believe me," he said pridefully, "you'll never have a tantrum again." I thought he'd go on and on in a tantrum of his own, but he left me alone, insisting I remain in the kneeling position where I'd landed. I didn't dare move. Every second felt like an hour. The floorboards dug into my knobby knees. I assumed, as kids do, that I was to blame. An eternity later, my mom came in to set me free from my restless and cramped position. I dreaded the next time I might do something that would provoke his temper.

As I continue to look at Chris's baby book with each of his birthday party invitations inside, I remember how my otherwise fearless toddler became fearful around anyone in costume. So, the Easter Bunny, clowns, and parade characters turned some of the fun upside down. When Christopher was afraid, I couldn't bear it. Like me, he was sensitive. And like me, he experienced his feelings deeply, so he wasn't just scared—he was frightened. In many ways, I love that about us. I've come to see it as a gift to get to experience life so fully. However, as Chris's mother, I would do everything in my power to protect him from feeling the shame of being different or from having to entertain any fear.

In the coming months, I try to take care of myself like never before. I rely on the resources I have used for a long time. I take my meds, talk to my therapist regularly, and get to extra self-help meetings for alcoholics and family members who have been impacted by alcoholism. I add monthly massages, write to Christopher often, and try to spend time with friends even when I'd rather isolate. Friends suggest grief groups for bereaved parents, but I already have a built-in support network at these meetings. And yet, my grief evokes estrangement from other people regardless of the setting I'm in.

After talking about how ceaselessly I miss Christopher, one afternoon at a meeting a man approaches me on my way out the door. "Now, Sally, you do have two children who are still alive, right? I don't want you to forget that." I was taken aback by his comment. No matter how well-intentioned, I hadn't asked for his input.

"I sure do, Hank. Yup, thanks, gotta run!" I keep walking. *Thanks but no thanks. I have not forgotten about my two living children,* I whisper to myself. But I do want to talk about the child I lost as much as I want without it making people uncomfortable.

The good news is that I'm starting to share in Joe's inclination not to care about what people think—or say. I hope, at some point, to be able to regain an interest in what is happening with other people because my tolerance for other people's problems has become limited. Good thing I'm still off work because whatever large stores of empathy I used to possess appear to have evaporated.

I cry all the time—in the car, on the couch, in a fetal position, and generally alone. The only way to help someone understand what it feels like to lose a child would be to let them cut through my flesh, dig through my guts down beneath the bone to the core of me, and rip out my broken heart and lay it in front of them. If I cry in Joe's presence, it's silently while we're watching TV and holding hands. Joe cries openly, and I prefer to sob in private. We approach things differently and always have, so that helps us respect the fact that we will each grieve our own way. If Joe sees that I'm crying, even though I've tried to hide it, he'll ask me about what brought it on. I usually don't have the energy to explain what caused the latest surge of emotion. I just need to feel through it alone. While we share in the fact that it would be impossible for either of us to love Chris any more than we do, grief is a lonely road. Neither of us has the bandwidth to support the other. We are just holding on.

Anything at all might trigger the pain. I can't anticipate what will set it off. William chuckling under his breath, sounding exactly like him, going to the oral surgeon where he had his wisdom teeth taken out and charmed the nurses by bringing them donuts the next day to say thank you, driving past any local landmarks where I picked him up or dropped him off. There are landmines at every turn. I'm not ashamed of being catapulted from my default sad state into surges of overwhelming grief, but I feel the pressure to be both sad and "strong." Whatever that might look like. Even though William often sees me lying on the couch in my nightgown, I try not to let him see me cry while hypocritically wishing he would show me tears of his own.

One afternoon, I step into the bath, sprinkling my eucalyptus bath oil into the hot running water, and spot a little black spider who appears at the bathroom window. I used to be terrified of spiders. Each of my children inherited my squeamishness. But seeing this little spider, I recall how during a recent phone session with another medium, she told me Chris would show me spiders because he knew it would grab my attention. I'd taken it with a grain of salt, but Christopher was so provocative, it's exactly what he would do. For impact. Maybe he's trying to make sure I have really learned what he was trying to teach me while he was here—to turn fear on its head.

So, I sink down into the steamy water and say, "Awwwwww hiiiiii baby," as opposed to immediately running from the bathroom. I imagine myself in conversation with the little spider, as if he is Charlotte in Charlotte's Web, squeaking out, "Hey, Momma, don't freak out. It's just me saying hello."

I'm less afraid, but I'm not ready to get out of the tub and get any closer to it. I remember the last time I touched my son. I reached out my hand to hold his in mine, and he let me, just for a moment. Has he truly just shown up for me this way? I want to see it as a sure sign from him, proof that his spirit can present itself to me in different forms. I want so much to feel him close that I am willing to go beyond seeing this little spider as a sign and personify it as my son. If the little spider was actually my son, I would touch him, knowing that in spider form he would have to quickly crawl away. The "ick" in my mind is suddenly replaced by a sweet warmth like honey. Christopher knew how to get my attention, and he still does.

A friend of mine recently asked me what my signs are for

my son. When I began to tell him all the ways I draw upon to call him to me, I realize they are everywhere. In sunflowers, lighthouses, and feathers. Is being on the lookout for signs another act of desperation, like needing to believe in Heaven? All I know is that being open and willing to think there could be an afterlife is offering me a pathway to hope. Signs are as close as I can get to evidence that my heart is still connected to my son's and that life goes on. An ache and the second-guessing creeps back in. It requires some crazy faith to conclude Chris is sending me signs, but in this moment, I choose to believe.

Are you really there? I try to listen for him so I don't topple into the darkest places I've gone. I sense him trying to reassure me that I am a good mom, that I didn't fail him, that no one could have saved him. I can almost hear him. "Mom, how can you doubt me? You know I have a way of making things happen. It's like magic."

I lower myself deeper into the bath, letting the water soak into my skin and ease the tension in my jaw and neck. I know I'm living in a state of wishful thinking that my beautiful boy could embody a spider just so that I'd be able to have him close. But I won't survive unless I find a way to know he's still here. I turn to take another look at the little spider. I tell Chris I love him and dunk underwater. While my baths are comforting, they also evoke pain and regret. I'm in water and I lost him to water. I lift my head to see that he's skittering out of sight. *See you later, my darlin' boy.*

nine

*I*t's May, and I wasn't prepared for the way Mother's Day would pull me under. Despite beginning to have faith that Christopher is doing great wherever he is, his absence blares like a siren. Joe, trying to make everyone happy, wants us to come to his golf club for brunch. Caroline, always looking for an excuse to go out to a fancy brunch and put on a dress, is driving in from school in Wisconsin. She has been reluctant to talk about her brother or have us talk about him. I understand. Chris took up all the oxygen in a room and continues to. Especially hard is when the mention of Chris's name results in her historically tough dad becoming wracked by sobs. Will and I are dragging but don't argue with the plan. William won't talk about Chris either, but he isn't talking much at all. I've never enjoyed dressing up, but now it is an undertaking. If it weren't for Joe, I don't know that I would show up anywhere. I'm like a little girl building a blanket fort so she doesn't have to venture outside her cocoon. I can't find safety.

Sitting at a corner table looking out over varied shades of green on the golf course, I'm glad I came. The part of me that's here takes pleasure in being together as a family, even though just us four feels strange. Being from a larger family, a family of four never seemed complete. I pushed for a third child, even after

I miscarried. Looking across the table at my two living children, their pale blue eyes and willingness to celebrate this day, I am filled with gratitude. But the ever-present yearning for Chris is extra heavy today.

Where are you? I'd always wished I had a microchip for my boy—and I need one now. I look up at the clouds collecting in the sky as we leave the club, hoping for a sign. A heart-shaped cloud, a ray of sunlight. If I only knew he could hear me and feel what's in my heart, maybe it would keep the encroaching self-pity away. I think about how the four of us stood out in the middle of the playfields near our home, releasing lanterns into the night sky for Chris's birthday a month ago. None of us said a word as we watched the wind carry each of our lanterns until they turned into pinpricks of light we could barely make out. I just wanted the lanterns to come back. Now the four of us stand in the parking lot, taking in this beautiful day, and hesitate to go anywhere as if we're waiting for him. We hug and depart into our caravan of separate cars—Caroline heading back up to school, William joining me in mine, and Joe taking his.

Joe has been talking to mediums regularly. One of them recently told Joe that Chris admitted feeling bad about never thinking twice. Yet that was part of his charm. He lived completely in the moment without any consideration of consequences. As Joe and I have often joked, for Chris, there was only "now" and "not now." Joe tells me he just met a medium and that I need to talk to her. Despite her busy schedule, he convinces her to set up a reading for my birthday. I like her from the start. Toni's loud New Jersey accent flies out of my phone. She tells me she's sorry she's late for the reading, but her house is a "shit show" and she can't wait to tell me that she's crazy about my son. Apparently, he likes hanging out at her house and has been since Joe's reading with her a few weeks before. I have my notepad out and am ready to begin writing things down, but it's not easy, as she's all over the place. I hear about her home full of a bunch of dogs and a bunch of children who won't go to bed on time. No wonder Chris is around.

"Sally, he's here laughing at our chaos. This is different. I am going to do a different kind of reading for you. Okay?" Before I can get a word in, just as I'm wondering if this is for real and whether we should forget the whole thing, she says, "He's an old soul, charismatic, funny. He communicates with you through music. Do you like country music?" This gives me pause since I haven't always, but I do lately. "Okay, so Sally, this is what's different. I have to tell you about my child, Zaralena. She insane, she's five years old, and she has the gift." I begin to relax. I like this lady. She's refreshing. "Sally, Zara feels Chris too. She drives me nuts because she never wants to go to school. Chris tells me that's what he did to you. He's laughing, especially about how I've been bribing her to make her go. Since I've given in and let her stay home, he tells me he used to get away with staying home too. He wants you to know that he needed you to nag him. He didn't tell you enough, but he's thanking you now."

It's growing dark outside, so I turn on the light and continue writing across a new page. "The way you loved Chris was different. You broke the chain from your dad. Chris is your angel." I can't believe it. I keep getting the same message, and it's only been four months. I ask Joe to tell me more about his readings, wondering if this is just something that mediums say, and he tells me the messages he's been getting are completely different without reference to angels at all. Chris is my angel—I already knew that. I just have to stop questioning my own gut. When our time is up, I tell Toni how much it feels like Chris is right here, and before I can ask her how she gets paid, she interrupts, "Oh, he's here all right. He gets a kick out of hanging out with us in our craziness." She pauses for air and asks, "Sally, were you asleep when he drowned?"

My heart flips. A familiar punch to the gut stops me in my tracks. What if he was afraid or calling out for me while I lay sleeping? He needed me, and I wasn't there for him. I start to go to my darkest place, pull myself back, and then reluctantly admit, "I must have been sleeping at the time."

"Well, when he passed, he found his way back into your body where he could hear your heart beating. When he was dying, he turned over to lie in the same position he was in when you first carried him."

I can't speak. Tears pour from my eyes. I am a bit freaked out, but a feeling of peace washes over me. I thank her profusely, get off the phone, and try to absorb what she's just told me. I consciously try to release the painful images of my son's departure that have plagued me and replace them with the increasing comfort that he will always be a part of me. That I don't have to let him go. I close the screen door to the deck before heading up to bed, catching the windchimes' peaceful music. They are one of my favorite gifts we received after Chris died. My mom hung them by our door, and the soothing sound returns him home.

After the reading, I continue to write to Christopher. It helps me process my grief and meet my need to capture all that he packed into his twenty-one years. When Toni shared about her daughter, who sounds so much like Chris, it brought me back to his early school days. I remember my first inkling that he was struggling was at his kindergarten conference when the teacher expressed concern that he didn't know all his letters. By first grade, we had gotten him a tutor who taught him how to read well, but focus didn't come easily to my busy boy.

Back then, diagnoses of ADD were given 50 percent less frequently than they would be just eight years later. In the early 2000s, despite living in a privileged community with a progressive school system, we were ahead of the curve. I advocated to get him tested but then waited over a year for that to happen. Once we got the results, they were hard to interpret. The evaluation suggested we consider medication but did not provide a diagnosis. Why would they suggest medicating my child unless he met the diagnosis? I later learned the school was reluctant to diagnose children because they'd have to pay to provide services.

I started taking Christopher to see a child psychologist. Caroline, six, and William, two, would accompany me to his appointments and wait for him in the waiting room. Joe was working fifteen-hour days six days a week as a car dealer. I was generally overwhelmed but trying to help my child, who hadn't been easy for me to understand. When the psychologist implied that I was to blame for Chris's inability to focus and that he didn't need medication, just more attention from me, I took his recommendation seriously. I blamed myself and tried to spend more time with him, but his only desire was to be with his friends, especially since William, six years younger than Chris, often required my attention. Caroline was generally lost between her two brother's demands, and I was just grateful that she didn't appear to need me the same way. Chris easily became impatient and would end up making our lives miserable unless I'd let him go. Years later, I found out that the psychologist was no longer in business for some kind of unprofessional conduct. This first foray into asking for outside help marked the dawning of a feeling of futility that the help I sought would either not be forthcoming or would make things worse instead of better. It reinforced my inclination to conclude that it was all up to me and that I was failing.

School continued to be a challenge for Chris, and he became more of a challenge to me. We spent more money to consult with an outside ADD specialist. As Joe and I sat in his office awaiting test results for ten-year-old Christopher, we filled out ADD questionnaires for ourselves. Joe turned to me and said, "You have ADD, Sal. You over-focus. It's your fault he probably has it."

"*Me?*" I exclaimed. My husband and I were both pretty run down. He, from his work, and me from my kids. There never seemed to be enough of us to go around, so we easily fell into the blame game. I looked over at Joe's sheet. "How many boxes did *you* check?"

"I didn't check *every* box," he replied.

I raised an eyebrow and shot him a dirty look. "Honey, if you check just five of the twenty boxes, you have it. *I* only checked a couple. I think I'm just a doer but then I burn myself out."

"I checked eighteen," he reported sheepishly. I knew Joe couldn't see that what was happening here was more in his genes than mine. But this was not the time for this insight or for me to point the blame back in his direction.

Attention deficit is indisputably a McQuillen trait. Suddenly every McQuillen I'd ever met flashed before my eyes. Joe's sister Pat's messy car and distractibility, his brother Billy's willingness to take a dare. Much about Joe that I'd been baffled by began to make sense: Joe never seeing the laundry basket waiting to be brought up the stairs or placing his dishes in the sink and then being distracted by something else before they could make their way into the dishwasher. I'm compulsive and have no choice but to see things through. I was relieved there was an explanation for my boy's behavior. I no longer had to grasp at straws. Any denial

I'd had slipped away. I now had a definitive framework for understanding both my husband and my son.

When Chris was conclusively diagnosed with ADD and learning disabilities, it provided some hope. ADD was just beginning to garner more attention. The diagnosis helped explain his trouble focusing, as well as his impulsive behavior. I sought out every book about ADD I could find. Joe and I did not take Chris's new child psychiatrist's suggestion to try a stimulant lightly and were disappointed by the results. My already skinny child, who hated to go to bed, found that the medication suppressed his appetite and made falling asleep even more difficult. I questioned the meds but held out hope for the miracle some parents reported. I just wanted him to start to feel better about himself. I knew his self-esteem was beginning to plummet.

When Chris began to be pulled out of the main classroom more often, he felt the stigma. There weren't yet many kids getting directed to special resource classrooms. He hated speech therapy and eventually gave it up. He was self-conscious about being in any way different, and the draw to be a part of things was powerful. I fought Christopher's shame off as if it were my own, pushing it all further down.

Of the two or three medications Chris tried, one of them managed to reduce his provocative behavior toward his siblings and his increasing restlessness. He was constantly inciting arguments if he was home, incapable of keeping himself entertained, so any relief on this front was welcomed. I wondered if those negligible benefits were worth the fact that he didn't eat much and stayed up later than he should. Just getting him to take his medication regularly on a full stomach was a challenge, but I tried.

Unfortunately, his teachers didn't understand ADD, or Chris, for that matter. He was provided with more resources to support his learning differences, but he wasn't good at self-advocacy, especially since it brought more attention. I suspected his teachers were impatient with him because his lack of focus could seem like disrespect. His fifth-grade homeroom teacher told me, "I can't tell whether Chris can't do it or whether he just won't," when it came to his schoolwork. It felt to me as if he was suggesting my son was a "bad boy." I requested that he seat Chris in the front of the room rather than in the back to facilitate capturing his attention. I had to admit that I hadn't been able to get him to comply with my directions, so I'm not sure why I thought his teachers could.

"Sweetie, don't forget to brush your teeth," I'd call every morning before school.

No reply.

Several minutes later, after helping William tie his shoes and making sure Caroline was ready, I'd have to repeat myself in a more irritable tone, "Sweetie, we have to go . . . please brush your teeth!"

When this inevitably got us nowhere, I'd scream, "BRUSH your teeth right NOW!"

Chris would finally look up at me, wide-eyed. "What's the big deal, Mom? Why are you yelling at me?"

Annoyed with him for not listening and with myself for resorting to yelling, I'd feel helpless. The older he got, the less he could be tamed. Raising him was humbling. He was a force. I'm not sure he ever did what he was told.

In my honest moments, I can admit to myself the ways Chris scared me. Like my dad, he could change the energy in our home. Sitting on the staircase as a little girl, I'd peer into the kitchen to assess my dad's mood when he came home from work and headed straight for the liquor cabinet. His shadowy moods would affect my well-being, just as Chris's developing irritability and defiance were beginning to affect mine and everybody else's.

I wonder exactly what God was trying to teach me as I raised him. Before now, one of the most painful lessons of my life was to let go of Chris while he was still here. His constant quest to be free meant trying to keep him close, which was like throwing a bridle on a wild horse. I thought there would come plenty of opportunities when he got older for us to spend more time together because, although he was my wildest child, I adored spending time with him. His presence was deeply soothing to me. I longed for even a minute with him and was certain the future held more of those minutes.

Instead, he's gone. My grief is equal in power to my love—fierce and constant.

*T*he month of May signals the coming conclusion of a school year in my maternal brain. Getting to the other side of Mother's Day, too, has me anticipating longer days and added light and color bursting from the earth. Chris's friends are graduating or heading home from school. But I exist in a gray and faded world where even the most glorious magnolia blossoms and lush green leaves showing off in the neighboring trees appear dull. I want my baby home too.

I'm often awash in crisp memories and longing. The longing becomes so powerful that I picture my boy pulling into the driveway, his slender brown arm waving from the window of his jeep, bright green eyes catching mine. And then he slips away. I'm still here and he's not, and I no longer know who I am if I can't be his mother. A huge chunk of my identity, my role, my purpose has been stripped from me.

Will's lacrosse game falls on a Tuesday. I am not able to go watch him play, and I feel awful about it. I want to show up for him every chance I get, despite knowing I will run into people and can't anticipate what they'll say when they see me. It exhausts me just to contemplate it. I need to pace myself better. I am easily overwhelmed as my grief smothers me, making it hard to show up to be the cheerleader I have always been for William. Being a mother has defined me for twenty-two years, and now a third of my heart has been excised from my chest. Without Christopher here, I can't get my bearings—nothing holds me in place.

The morning after Will's game, the rain lightly sprinkles, and the sky is gray. My inclination is to stay home in my Lanz nightgown, to retreat into a cozy corner and cry, whereas Joe insists upon keeping himself more busy than usual. Instead, I drag myself to a board meeting for an organization that brings speakers to our town. The meeting is called to order, and the first item on the agenda is to introduce ourselves to one other since the organization has recently grown. With at least sixty people in the room this could take a while. Beginning on the other side of a large table, a petite woman in a tennis outfit stands up and softly announces, "Hi, I'm Jane Shelton. I'm the mother to three boys, ages four, six, and seven, and I'm the liaison for Central Elementary School in Evanston. This is my first year on the FAN board."

I'm not sure whether I am breathing as I hold my head up on high alert. The bright white lighting in the large classroom we're filling starts to buzz. It's too bright in here. The walls close in. I'm wondering if there is a way out of this, but I realize if I stand up now, I'll only be calling attention to myself. I'm consciously trying not to bounce in my chair as I look around and listen to each woman introduce herself while trying to formulate how I'll talk about my children as my turn approaches. All eyes turn my way, and I grab hold of the table in front of me and push back my chair.

"Hello, I'm Sally McQuillen. I am a mother of three children, my oldest whom I lost nearly five months ago was twenty-one, my daughter is nineteen, and my youngest son is sixteen. I am a liaison to the Erika's Lighthouse Board." I'm so relieved the words came out. I will never not claim my son. I fall back into my chair shakily and feel a chill. *Thank you, Chris, for giving me the strength.* This hijacking of my emotions is happening to me more regularly. I'll think I have it together and then something happens to pull me into a tailspin. I can't think straight, and in fight or flight on steroids, I'm reeling. As I listen to other people talk, I realize I took for granted so much the privilege of being a mother to each one of my children. I look around at the women, many just starting out on their parenting journey, and wish I was just starting out too. I could do it all better than I have and find a way to save my son. *Sally, you know that's not true,* I tell myself as I try to pay attention, but my heart has left the room.

When I meet with my therapist Ellen the next day and tell her about the ways I become flooded with feeling, she educates me about how trauma works, explaining that sights, sounds, words, and smells can trigger unprocessed grief. Since there are so many ways my central nervous system is getting activated, she recommends EMDR (eye movement desensitization and reprocessing) therapy and makes a referral.

The next week, I'm sitting in my jeep in the parking lot of the new therapist's office, encouraging myself to get out of the car for my first appointment. Once I locate the office at the end of a long hallway, I sit in the waiting room summoning strength. I'd rather run than feel more, but I know I need to do something to address the layer of panic on top of the pain. I sit in the corner of a red corduroy couch, nervously awaiting the therapist's questions. We go through some formalities, and then Carol, who looks like a grown-up Cindy-Lou-Who with her big blue eyes and blond bob, asks brightly, "So, tell me what brings you here?"

I pull my jacket tightly around me and start in, "Well, since my son Christopher died in January, my world has been rocked. I often flash back to what I imagine were his last moments. I picture him in the cold water without me there to comfort him. I fight it, but I picture him suffering and become terrified. Like a magnet, I'm pulled into haunted places against my will. I try to stop the intrusive thoughts, but they keep coming, and I fall into a place of extreme powerlessness. I'll be opening the refrigerator or doing an errand when I hear the word 'Noooo' fly from my mouth as I fight against the truth of what happened. My child is dead." I swallow and pause, suddenly worried that this sweet Carol might not be able to handle what I'm bringing her way. She sits forward in her chair, fluffs up her bangs, and surprises me by saying, "Well, then let's get to it."

And we do. After getting more history from me, she encourages me to move my eyes along the flashing lights she holds in front of me as she has me review the most painful mental pictures I've been holding.

Each session after that is emotionally exhausting, but I feel the fog lifting, the terror and guilt subsiding, and a lightening in my body after the tears have poured out of me. I show up, being willing to be broken open, and thankfully these sessions somehow help me shift beyond the dark, eerie imagery of my son suffering. Just as I'd begun to do with Toni's reading that Chris came back to me as he passed, I superimpose a new picture in my mind's eye. I see Chris making an ascension into a glowing pool of light, where he feels the warmth of a love so deep it pulls him toward it. I see him also becoming a greater part of me. Being in therapy for as long as I have already and being committed to moving through this pain helps me. But each time I am so wrung out I can barely move afterward, and I re-enter a world of memories. I'm left longing for my child. Not just for the best version of him who loved with his whole heart but for the real Christopher who was always giving me trouble.

During Chris's middle school years, setting boundaries and limits with him got harder and harder. He wanted to spend more time, not less, with his friends. Each weekend he hounded me, "Mom, can I have a sleepover at Jack's?"

"No, honey. You had a sleepover last night, and I don't want you to get sick again. You need your rest."

"But Mom, Jack's dad said he would take us bowling. We'll sleep."

"Not this time, Christopher."

"Mom! Mom! Mom! His mom said yes already. I won't have any sleepovers next weekend."

He'd follow me as I walked away. He'd pound on the bathroom door after I went in and locked it behind me to try to stick to my guns. When I didn't come out and relent to his wishes, he'd head off to provoke his sister and brother. At times I was afraid he might seriously hurt Caroline or William with an unexpected punch, though more often I was concerned about how much he could hurt them with his words. He could be cutting and critical and inclined to start fights, hauling insults designed to bring them to tears. He couldn't help but relentlessly try to get me to give in to him. He had to be with his buddies. His siblings looked up to him so much, but I knew how hurtful this became to them. I admit to giving in to his demands more than I should have just to be able to protect them and grant the rest of us some peace. I started to become accustomed to living in a constant state of anxious anticipation of the next blow-up at home or problem at school as they occurred more frequently up through his years in junior high.

By the summer Chris was thirteen, he got into trouble with a group of bored adolescent boys roaming around our suburban Chicagoland town in a pack. They had thrown stones at the lights in the ground at a local elementary school, causing thousands of dollars of damage. Chris had to do community service and help pay to repair the lights. So, when the phone rang late on a Friday night, Joe picked up, mumbling, "What now?"

I sat up in bed, and Joe put his hand on my arm to prevent me from interrupting. "I'm sorry, but can you repeat that? Is everybody okay?" He turned away from me, and I stared at his tired eyes, trying to hear what the person on the other end of the phone was saying.

". . . Okay, good. Glad to hear. You're home now? D'you want us to come get him? . . . if you're sure. Okay, see you in the morning." He nodded my way. "Let's talk to them then. You got it. See you at ten."

"Oh my God, honey, what's going on?"

"He's fine, Sal," Joe assured me. "He and his friends got into some booze. One of the kids got so intoxicated that the others freaked out and called the paramedics."

My breath seized up in my lungs. "Are you sure he's all right? Was that Jake's mom? I thought he was spending the night at Jake's dad's house."

"They snuck out of Jake's dad's and broke into his mom's house through the back screen because they knew she'd be out. There were six of them, and they got ahold of some vodka. Luckily the kid who drank too much is okay. We need to show up tomorrow with the police and scare these kids if they aren't scared already."

Joe barely blinked an eye. He was essentially unfazed, as the incident came as no surprise to him. His mother had raised ten kids while his dad worked on the railroad. As the youngest, Joe had been a troublemaker. A charming, dimpled-faced Irishman, he liked to laugh and tell story after story with his brothers and sisters about all the antics he proudly got away with. To him, what Chris and his friends had done was something he and his buddies would have done too.

I didn't take it as well as Joe. I was relieved that Chris's friend was all right, but I was worried. They were only thirteen years old. Joe had been a hellion, but so had I. At thirteen, I'd already gotten drunk, blacked out, and made a fool of myself on at least several occasions. My father's volatile moods, which were such a source of fear for me, were rooted in his alcoholism. I hadn't made the connection between my dad's scary behavior and his alcoholism until after I'd begun drinking myself. Even knowing about it, I doubt I would have been able to steer away from alcohol's powerful allure. From the moment I snuck a lick off of the stopper of my dad's whiskey decanter, I awaited what it promised.

When I began drinking at thirteen, it offered relief I didn't know I needed. Or so I thought. Therefore, it wasn't hard to see the writing on the wall with my son. Christopher's enthusiasm had been dimming, and he'd started to run with a faster crowd. He wouldn't look at me or give me the time of day. Since he was my first, I didn't know how much of this was typical teenage acting out or a cause for fear my family legacy of alcoholism could not be broken. He could be seeking relief as I had for the familiar unease I often felt at his age before I was diagnosed with anxiety and depression. My heart pounded as I lay wide awake, staring up at the ceiling, while Joe immediately went back to snoring beside me. I became more motivated to try to spare my children from the disease and its fallout.

The morning after the phone call, we fell into what had become a predictable pattern. I prepped Joe so he'd emphasize to the boys how frightening the episode was and that it couldn't happen again. There also needed to be consequences. "Honey, we need to discipline him. I think we should stop allowing him to have sleepovers."

"I'm more than willing to share my experience as a recovering alcoholic, Sal. I've got this. Don't worry." My husband seized the opportunity to tackle this incident, assuring me he was going to use some scare tactics. However, I knew it would be hard for him to hold the line because Joe felt guilty for not being around much. He wanted to do whatever he could to make our children happy and make up for all his time away. Plus, he was often too wiped out to enforce the consequences I'd try to introduce and couldn't enforce myself.

Joe had always been more vocal with Chris about his history with alcohol, particularly about how wild he'd been. I deliberately chose not to speak with my kids about my drinking because I wanted to do anything I could to not condone underage drinking. I thought I was protecting him. I didn't realize I had not yet integrated my own differentness as a recovering alcoholic. I would have told people I was proud of it. Mostly, I knew how brutal a disease it could be and how fortunate I'd been to get sober against the odds.

Before we headed out the door I emphasized, "I want you to tell the boys about the dangers of alcohol abuse, but I don't think now is the time for me to reveal my own alcoholism. I don't want Chris to think I endorse his behavior. It feels like no matter what we do, he keeps heading for trouble."

"Don't get ahead of yourself on this," Joe cautioned as he tugged his sweatshirt over his broad shoulders. "It might be the first time he ever drank." Joe made good on his plan to pull in a few local police officers for effect. "They're going to help me deliver a message, but Sal," he said, "you've got to control him better. I can't be here every time this kind of shit happens."

Having grown up the youngest of ten kids with a father who'd financially provided for them all, he had a great appreciation for his father's hard work and long hours. He took pride in doing the same for us. For him, this achievement superseded the importance of running the household and managing the children. Like so many stay-at-home moms, I knew my role to be no less challenging or important. I hadn't planned on ending up in such traditional marital roles, yet when I'd attempted to work outside of the home, I hadn't been able to make it all work. The demands at home had been too great, and the financial compensation hadn't been worth it. I was glad I could "stay at home" for the most part, but I was also convinced, especially with the benefit of hindsight, that working outside of the home would have been easier for me. But doing both jobs full-time as so many women do, I might have snapped.

"Honey, I wish I could control him. I really do." I sighed as tears of frustration pricked at my eyes. "I've been trying so hard to prevent this from happening. I've read that the longer you wait before you start drinking, the less likely you are to become an alcoholic. I'm scared for Chris since addiction runs in both of our families. He's so impulsive and reckless it's impossible to handle him. I wish I knew what to do." My voice broke with emotion as I recognized my need to fight the outcome I feared.

Embarrassment washed over me as I remembered a time a few years back when I discovered another mom had been talking behind my back about my inability to control Chris. Apparently, a bunch of kids had gathered at her home for a party her daughter was having, and when she offered to drive them home, Chris ran off with a few friends. Her judgment stung badly because it seemed like I was being accused of being a bad mom. I tortured myself, beating myself up for not being able to manage him better. Reactive, I ended up going so far as to contact her and sarcastically thank her for her concern. I knew I'd gone overboard in my defense, telling her how much I appreciated how she had looked out for him "since God knows it takes a village to raise a child." It would take years before I would be able to see that this was my retaliation for the judgment I'd felt.

When we got to Jake's mom's house where Chris had spent the night, Jake's mother greeted us at the door in a bright sundress. Like Joe, she seemed mostly unaffected. Perhaps she was accustomed to this kind of thing since she had a bunch of older boys. Half-a-dozen boys and a few of their parents were there. Most of the kids lounged on the rug, looking pale and exhausted from lack of sleep and too much to drink. Joe somehow had gotten two police officers to show up. They arrived right after we got there, wearing their black Kevlar vests. We all gathered in the dining room.

The story came out that our sons had convinced a stranger at the gas station to buy them vodka. They had taken it back to the house where there was no adult supervision and took turns chugging from the bottle. When one of the boys passed out on the floor and they couldn't wake him, they called 911. Jake's mom arrived home soon after the boy had been treated at the hospital and had contacted us when it was concluded that he was all right.

Some of the parents saw the incident as typical teen experimentation. Joe took the lead and spoke with the boys in a serious tone. But the kids didn't seem to be listening. Even the presence of the cops didn't make the impact I'd hoped to see. I watched my son, who was fidgety and eager to get on with his weekend, concluding this hadn't scared him the way I imagined it would. I had better be more proactive. I needed to do better. I had to spare him from the shame and sadness I'd known. I had to come up with a plan that would prevent anything bad from happening.

eleven

The whole month of May has been filled with more EMDR sessions intermixed with celebrations and events. Tonight, we are heading to The Penguin Players Show. This will be extra heartbreaking, but nothing can keep me away. When Chris was at Northern Illinois University, he majored in Special Education. He wanted to work with children who learned differently. The day after Chris died, as my brother was helping to write Chris's obituary, he asked to whom donations could be directed. I replied immediately, "The Penguin Players Program and In Balance Ranch Academy." The year before, Chris encouraged me to come to watch a musical performance put on by a troupe of artists with special needs and their mentors (students from the special education department). Chris mentored a young man named Daniel for the first Penguin Players program of its kind in the country, which was designed for adults who have aged out of other programs. Daniel's parents are the founders of The Penguin Players, and they designate any donations we have raised in Christopher's honor to support the student volunteers who form the creative team behind the productions. This financial support is given to caring, enthusiastic student mentors in the form of Chris McQuillen Spirit Awards each semester.

Nearly a year and a half since that show, Joe and I decide to meet at this show since he'll be coming from the golf course. I oversleep, and I'm running late. Every time I've made this drive southwest through the cornfields, I've chuckled about the strong, cold winds that gain force the closer I get because of how Chris liked to joke that he'd ended up in the wind capital of the world for college. He hated the cold, but he loved NIU. Or should I say, he loved AKL, his fraternity home away from home.

This is the only time the sun has ever shone on my drive to NIU, so I take the top off my jeep, slather on some sunscreen, and pull my hair back in a ponytail. At first it feels good, the sun warming my arms as the breeze whips past. I fly through a yellow light that turns red on me and hope I don't get caught. That's what Chris would have done. We weren't so different after all—both liking our freedom and rebellion.

As I pass white barns in the distance beyond golden fields, I experience a flicker of joy. I'm going to see my boy! Then my stomach seizes. He isn't there. Goddamn it. A gust of wind blows the jeep so hard I start to imagine being carried above the fields, spinning into the air like the witch's house in *The Wizard of Oz*. I welcome being pulled closer to my boy. Is that where I might find him? I could join him in a sunlit sky and leave the world behind.

Clouds gather, and I'm still here, gripping the wheel, palms sweating. I try to comfort myself with the idea that Chris is doing great in Heaven, which is all a mother ever wants to be able to do. We like to brag. And I don't get to anymore. I talk to him, letting him know how proud I felt when I saw him by Daniel's side, guiding his dance steps, whispering his lines. I remember how surprised I was to see my son perform dressed up in a tuxedo with his hand gently placed on Daniel's back to direct him. I remember my excitement when I saw him walk on stage.

Ten minutes late, I pull into the parking lot next to Joe, who's just arrived too. We race inside the theater, where Daniel's mom is there to greet us. Daniel's parents put their hearts and souls into these performances, where mentors are partners, cheerleaders, and friends to the artists they mentor. We settle into our seats, and when the curtain rises, I smile and cry when I locate Daniel onstage with a new mentor by his side. As I watch the artists recite their lines and happily respond to the audience clapping at their jokes, I know this is the perfect way to honor our son's passion for the underdog. The highlight of the show is a solo beautifully sung by Daniel and the moving finale, where the entire cast and crew belt out the song "Don't Stop Believing" to a standing ovation.

The next evening after I've gotten into bed, I hear our yellow Labrador Cassidy creep up the stairs and begin to whine. *Is she okay?* I wonder, but I can't get out of bed. In a month I'll be going back to work, which concerns me. I am rarely not tired. I feel guilty enough to peek out my door to check on her. I have gone from practically ignoring her as a puppy (often brushing her aside with the inside of my calf) as I raced the kids off somewhere to fawning over her like I should have when she was a baby. Now she wanders into my room, looking up at me with her dark brown eyes and closing them when I take her soft ear in my hand and rub it.

I can't believe she is nearly eleven and only now beginning to slow down. When we first brought her home, I wanted her to be like our first Lab, Casey, a mellow puddle of mush. Instead, she was full of vinegar, leaping onto the counter to try to eat our goldfish, inadvertently turning on the kitchen faucet, and spilling water onto the floor in puddles. Her boxy head and latte color made me think (as I did with Chris), *Good thing you're so cute!* I'd call to her, "Come, Cassie, come!" and she'd look right at me and ignore me just as Chris had. She continues to be strong-willed, sneaking onto the couch at night, her cover blown by loads of white dog hairs woven into the pillows the next morning.

I adore her. She hasn't left my side since Chris died. Historically more aloof and independent, she now seems to intuit my need for comfort. Lately I'm sleeping in my room across from the master bedroom, where I have sought a hide-out from Joe's loud snores. I'm the princess and the pea. Cuddled in my childhood bed, I wrap myself in the softest of blankets and burrow my head into the silkiest pillow. I've done what I can to create a safe space. I keep essential oils on my bedside table, and before trying to get to sleep, I place droplets of mandarin oil into my palm and inhale.

I wake up as I often do, teeth clenched, heart racing, the muscles in my jaw tight as rope. I had another dream where I lost something. Where I am lost. I am someplace I have never seen before. Somehow, I know I'm away at college, even if the buildings and landscape appear entirely unfamiliar. In some of these dreams I find myself in old gothic buildings with dark, heavy wood doors and Hogwarts winding staircases leading me on without end. I am trying to find my classroom. I'm unprepared. There is always something I have left behind. I enter a modern maze with glass ceilings, late for an exam. I am anxious, berating myself for not knowing how to find my way. But I never do. Without exception, the same theme permeates the only dreams I remember. It doesn't take an analyst to figure out I'm condemned to search. I'm incomplete.

This last dream was so vivid, I'm still in it. People have asked whether Chris visits me in my dreams, but so far there have only been flickers of his beauty, glimpses of his face. This time, Christopher is a hawk. Gray, outstretched wings of an angel, bright green wide eyes zoom closer to me, and I feel him filling up the space. I wake up, trying to hold onto the feeling, no more ready to let go than I ever am. I am enthralled by the prospect that the hawk I spotted circling my jeep as I drove to the show yesterday may have been a sign from my free-spirited, soaring son. I think about how I would lift Christopher above my head when he was small. I'd hold him over me in an "airplane" flying as I brought his smiling face closer to mine.

I get dressed and stop at Starbucks on my way to Chris's grave. I've written amends to him in hopes that it will relieve me of the persistent negative self-talk I torture myself with, wishing I could have parented him with more confidence. I stand holding tightly to the page I've typed as it ruffles in the breeze and begin to read, "Christopher, our deep bond was always there even though I feared it wasn't secure because I couldn't pin you down. It was secure and will exist forever. I'm sorry I didn't always trust it. I'm sorry I became overwhelmed by your wildness and frustrated by your defiance. I wish I could have been less reactive when I was dealing with you. I wish I could have given you more of the structure that you needed but bucked. I'm sorry you inherited addiction from Dad and me. I am especially sorry that you had to feel my fear. I learned too late how letting go of fear could make our relationship better. I apologize for the times I was too anxious or depressed to be as emotionally present as you deserved. I wish I could have been more fun. I hated it when you were ever hurting, and I never wanted to be the cause of even an ounce of pain. I adore you, Momma."

I let my tears fall as I read. No one else is here in the cemetery, which makes it easier. I wipe my eyes as I let out a long sigh. I stand looking up at the sky, hoping Chris has heard me.

I hesitate before bending down to rub my hand across the letters engraved in his gravestone, pull my jacket tighter around me, and force myself to walk away. I want to make peace with the past, allow my guilt to lift and float away, knowing it will return with its black ooze of leftover regret for more release next time, where it will dissolve into forgiveness for myself, bit by bit. I pray that, over time, I can move beyond my guilt and suffering, make fear a stranger to me, and keep my heart open.

Driving off in my jeep, I realize it is here, looking at his face on his prayer card and listening to music, that I feel most connected to Chris. I turn up the volume on a Fleetwood Mac song as relief washes over me. They are one of the first bands I ever loved. I sing *Love in Store* out loud, feeling their voices meld together and recalling how young I was when I sat in my room studying each member of the band on their "Rumours" album cover.

I'm singing to Chris. I'm not in tune, but I don't care. His girlfriend Gali told me that when they were dating, he would sing "You Are My Sunshine" to her over the phone and "He Went to Paris" by Jimmy Buffet. "I have a terrible voice," he told her, "but I'm a great singer!" Smiling at the memory of this intimacy she shared, I pull up to a stop sign, and a dark shape enters my line of vision from the left. It is a hawk descending low enough for me to see its fluffy white underbelly speckled with brown. It shifts in flight, slowing down. I see this as Chris reassuring me that I'm forgiven, but I don't know if I can entirely let myself off the hook yet. The hawk rises higher and higher away until I can't see him anymore.

I'm taking a trip to Savannah with my only girl cousin, Anne. She grew up in France and now lives in the States temporarily.

We've always been quite close. Scheduled to go back in a few days, she called this morning. My aunt and godmother, her mother, is dying. She must fly to Paris in hopes of getting there in time. My aunt's been ill with cancer, but we're unprepared for this to be happening now. I try to absorb what she's telling me and consider flying in to support her. But Anne wants me to go to Savannah. I know she wants to spare me from having to attend another funeral on the heels of my loss. I feel guilty but want to respect Anne's needs.

I regret that Chris didn't have a lot of time with my Aunt Eda. They have so much in common, both shining stars driven and defined by their friendships, both beautiful, charismatic, magnetic personalities whose light we all clamored to have shine on us. Chris, the life of the party, and Aunt Eda, a gracious hostess. She loved to travel, and he loved adventure. They both loved horses and the West.

When I analyze it, as I am inclined to do, I think that both individuals who I wholeheartedly adored had demons in the form of anxiety and depression that they fought to keep at bay. It's not easy to shine so brightly. As I reluctantly pack for my now solo weekend away, I imagine *ma belle tante* (as I called her) soaking in cool, clear water in her pool in the French countryside. I see a clear image of her in my mind's eye— standing up, wrapping herself in a towel, and laying her hands on my shoulders as she did the day I got married. She looks right from her green eyes into my own, and I see that her pain has been washed away. No more cancer cramping the hands that wanted to dance across piano keys. She is softened, luminous, and free. The sunset melts from pink into orange liquid all around her. I want to digest her glow as if I could swallow its warmth and take it with me.

At the airport gate the next afternoon, I find a seat adjacent to a café and people-watch. A group of loud young women suddenly appears, collecting at the bar. One young woman stands out. I can't take my eyes off her. She's wearing dark, fitted jeans, a short black leather jacket, and a floppy hat. Normally I would think the outfit frivolous, but on her, it works, enhancing her sharp cheekbones and icy blue eyes. She's striking and, I'm guessing, is in her midthirties, but everyone looks young to me these days, so who knows?

This Kate Moss lookalike ends up sitting right next to me on the plane. Before takeoff, she giggles on the phone with a friend. I immediately like her and smile when she turns toward me. I open my book and think about how I've become different since Chris died. I want to sit quietly, enjoy my solitude, and read without being interrupted. Yet, I can imagine myself talking with her.

When she initiates conversation, I share more than I planned to. I tell her I'm heading to Savannah by myself. That my cousin and I had scheduled a girls' weekend, but she wasn't able to come last minute. The young woman points to some of the women on our flight, "We're all in a book group and just finished reading *Midnight in the Garden of Good and Evil,* so we decided to make it into a girl's trip. It's so good just to get time away from the kids."

I hear words fly out of my mouth before I can stop them. I feel at ease enough with her to open up. "That's amazing. I wish I had taken trips more often when my kids were young. My aunt has just died," I share, sensing her receptivity. I tell her about my cousin, who was going to be on this trip with me and just arrived in Paris in time to say goodbye.

"I'm so sorry for your loss. I think it's important to have time to grieve and time to explore new places." She says this with such warmth and openness that I go on, "My aunt was special to me, and I'm so relieved my cousin got there in time." Losing my aunt hasn't even sunk in yet, and although I feel sad, I also feel relieved to talk about it. She takes her phone from her lap and places it in her bag, turning closer, so I continue, "I have also always wanted to visit the southern sights, wander around the squares, and, now that I'll be there by myself, I'm going to also spend some time working on my book."

Before I realize it, I'm at that uncomfortable crossroads again. Do I tell her what I'm writing about? Since it already feels like I have known her for a lot longer than I have, I go there, albeit warily, "I am also grieving my son. After I lost my twenty-one-year-old in January, a friend encouraged me to begin writing. I am hoping to take my journal entries and turn them into a memoir."

I watch her porcelain face, and her eyes spark with a refreshing interest in lieu of pity. She doesn't turn away. "Wow, I bet writing is a great way to process your feelings." Her dark hair falls back from her face as she turns to me and takes my hand in hers, her hat now tucked at her feet. She grasps my hand for a moment, and I squeeze hers back.

I relish her response. She remains open and interested, so I go on. "I feel so connected to my son through my writing. After losing him, I am doing things I wouldn't otherwise have done," I explain. I tell her about the writing retreat I'm going to attend the following weekend and how Joe is writing a book of his own. "Knowing him, he'll probably get it published before I've even started." As I say this, I realize I'm envious of my husband's unshakable confidence.

We talk and talk, easily continuing this conversation about

how Joe and I have different approaches to our writing but we want to honor Chris and carry a message that helps other people. It's so refreshing to neither feel like I need to take care of someone emotionally nor fear that she'll change the subject immediately. She listens with sincere interest.

"What exactly is the message, do you think?" she asks.

I pause because I don't know where to start. There is so much I am discovering as I write through my grief.

"I feel like it's about what it's like to grieve a child, how to let go of fear and guilt, and take better care of myself." I hesitate, and then my conviction surprises me, "That love never dies. That's the real message."

"Oh, this is an important message. I wish my mom had had it when she lost her sister ten years ago. She's still struggling. Death wasn't something that was talked about."

I listen closely as she describes how her mother's unresolved grief has affected her and how she is talking more openly about difficult feelings with her own young daughter. She is speaking my language.

"I know that death makes people uncomfortable, but everybody has to die, so wouldn't it be great if it didn't feel so taboo to talk about it?" She nods, and I go on. "I want to be able to write about my pain from inside it and express all the love I have for him. Now I understand that there is nothing more important than love." I'm emotional as I share, and the young woman asks, "Have you ever heard of *A Course in Miracles*? I've been meaning to read it for a while."

I can't believe it. This whole conversation feels orchestrated by Chris's spirit. I've known about *A Course in Miracles* for years. The course emphasizes the importance of moving from fear toward love, which is exactly what I need to do now more than ever. Just recently I'd found out a friend of mine is teaching it—so what are the chances that this is coming up now?

"I'm getting the idea that my son wants me to take it," I tell my new friend Monika.

Before I know it, the plane is making its descent. We exchange numbers, and I tell her that I'm going to buy the book. She promises to take it down from her shelf when she gets home. She pulls her seat upright and asks me a question I've been longing to hear, "What was your son like?"

My biggest fear now is that people will forget Christopher. I hate that when people die, we often stop talking about them. Chris is so very much alive for me, so this, I think, will always be my favorite question, and yet I struggle to find the words. How can I possibly capture his spirit?

"He was beautiful. He was challenging. He was able to be both cool and big-hearted. He kept me on my toes from the very beginning, and I am so grateful for every minute of it. I know that he was meant to be my son and I was meant to be his mother."

She smiles and I hug her goodbye.

"It's been a pleasure," I call out as we part ways. Once settled in at the hotel, there's a text message from her thanking me for sharing myself. I realize, in that moment, that that's exactly what Chris would have done. He would have connected and made an impact quickly as if he already knew that life is short and love is the only thing that matters in the end.

twelve

I can't wait to get out and explore Savannah. I walk along the city's old cobblestone streets draped by a canopy of trees. Drawn here by the allure of its great oak trees with their shelter of Spanish moss hanging from broad branches, I feel small in the shadowy presence of their long-armed embrace. I wish I could climb high and sit perched above the world like I did as a little girl, surveying my neighborhood from the tree house in my backyard. I'd climb to the top, where I could see far beyond my home to the neighboring yards, and let my imagination run. The grace and strength of the wide-trunked, twisted old trees make me feel as if I'm sitting in my grandmother's lap. It helps me begin to know I'm not as alone as I tended to feel as a child and have felt in my grief.

My therapist recently asked me to picture myself being comforted by someone. Who would it be? What would it feel like? My grandmother, Nanny, came to mind. In her floral dress and pearls, she accompanied me to wash my hands when I was small. She entered the tiny bathroom behind our kitchen and stood by my side, turning on the faucet to make sure the water was warm. She tucked my little hands inside her own soft, wrinkled ones, massaging them with soapy suds.

Whenever I was with Nanny, I felt wrapped in satin. She saw

the best in me. She was keenly interested in what I could reveal to her about myself. I welcomed her questions and cherished her undivided attention. Because she was asthmatic and had had a heart attack in her fifties, I approached each visit with her as if it might be the last. She lived to be one hundred, and I felt the warmth of her adoration until the very end. Even after she took a fall and I wondered if she might forget me, she continued to radiate the same warm affection my way. It was exactly how I must have looked at Christopher, who was like water slipping through my fingers. I was aware of trying to prolong the moments, knowing he'd soon be on his way. Thinking about Nanny's and Christopher's smiles while watching the light cast shadows in the trees, I can transcend my sadness for a moment. I become part of something greater. I am lifted even as I falter.

I end up along Bay Street by the riverwalk when it begins to grow dark. As I head down the steep stone steps to the water, I wonder, *What would Christopher want to see if he was here with me?* When I look up to get my bearings, a full moon glows out from behind the mist. Deep silvery gray and purple clouds move across the moonlight. I allow the light of the moon and the chords of a distant guitar to guide me back to the city market. There, I find an outdoor table where I listen to a band play Lynyrd Skynyrd's "Simple Man." The lyrics land like never before from a mother to her son, reminding him to follow his heart and not to forget he is being looked after. I let the music wash over me, noticing how Chris is becoming a conduit to my someone up above, bringing me closer to a Higher Power that is a source of light and the strength I need to live another day without him.

Back home from Savannah, with summer upon us, I begin to think about returning to work in July and what I need to do to take care of myself before I go back. That week I contact an energy healer named Ariel Hardy. I didn't even know such a thing existed until recently. I have been listening to Ariel's morning meditations for a few weeks on my morning drive to Starbucks, and I'm ready for her help. I'm not exactly sure what's happening, but maybe the protective layer of shock I've been in is floating away because my heartache now engulfs me. It dawns on me more every day that not only have I lost my son, but I will have to spend the rest of my life without him. I hadn't gotten that far until now. I am processing slowly, one layer of loss at a time, and this reality is beyond my ability to fathom.

I can barely feel anything other than devastated. One of the only exceptions is when I am with my niece, Emma. At two, she is a sunbeam with bouncy curls and dimpled fingers, so when I can be in the moment with her, I access joy. But mostly I am consumed by grief and concerned about my own living children: William, who has been too shut down to talk about his feelings of devastation, and Caroline, who gets angry at the mention of Chris's name.

When I have my session with Ariel, I explain the predicament I'm in. "I don't think Chris would want me to feel this bad, but if I'm not suffering, it might seem to him like I don't love him as deeply as I do." I wring my hands after putting her on speaker.

"Yes, I understand," Ariel says softly. Her voice is ethereal, and I form a picture in my mind of a little fairy orbiting above the phone. "But your pain can actually be a barrier to feeling your son around you. Your energy has to continue to move through you, and this suffering could be holding you back."

I interrupt, "Ohhhh, I don't want *anything* to interfere with having him close. What do I need to do? Where do we start?"

"Well, before we begin, Sally, is it possible you could be blaming yourself for his death?"

I confess to her that intellectually I know I could not have saved him but that, yes, I blame myself, and my powerlessness to prevent his death gnaws at me.

"That might be blocking you too," she suggests. "Let's get you out of your own way. We need to get you to accept things as being exactly how they are meant to be. Christopher, can you help me with your mom?"

Immediately, I feel his presence in the room. Ariel asks me to stand up from my chair and let my shoulders drop from my ears. She tells me to let go of self-blame, to become fluid, and to stop resisting so I can be open to the love that exists between us.

"Sally, it's all right to be crying one minute and laughing the next. Stop fighting what is. Go ahead and feel your pain, but stop judging it or trying to get rid of it. That's what is keeping you stuck. Picture Christopher right now as if he's climbing up a ladder. He is stepping toward you to chip away at the critical voice inside your head. He is working his way down from the top of your crown into your shoulders and neck to break up your knots and let light in."

My head begins to ache and tingle as I take in her words. The sensation extends into my arms and fingers, and as it does, I imagine my pain cracking into pieces and falling away. After several minutes of listening to Ariel, my head buzzes, and tears come into my eyes. I feel something clearing inside of me. Intuitively, I know this time with her has been healing. There is a shift in my body, and I feel lighter.

"Is my son still with me?" I ask.

"He's here," Ariel says. "He has his arm outstretched and is taking a dramatic bow."

I smile. That sounds exactly like him.

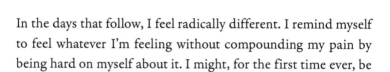

In the days that follow, I feel radically different. I remind myself to feel whatever I'm feeling without compounding my pain by being hard on myself about it. I might, for the first time ever, be developing some self-compassion.

There are a few more weeks of June left before I head back to work at the outpatient addiction center. The most important thing coming up is a writing retreat I signed up to attend in Montana to learn how to turn my writing to Chris into a memoir. I felt like Chris led me to it because of the synchronicity of realizing the founder's life and mine had already intersected. Meanwhile, I want to be sure to preserve some necessary self-care in the form of self-help meetings before I throw myself back into work. I don't want to let my self-help meeting attendance fall off as it did when I was busily raising my three children and told myself that talk therapy alone was enough to keep me sober. I had taken for granted that meetings provide an anchor for me, and now they give me a place to express my grief and find spiritual solace. While I got lucky that I didn't resume drinking during that time, I was running in never-ending circles to stay afloat and essentially out of my body for years, busyness and distraction having become my new "drug of choice."

Time stood still the summer between Chris's eighth grade and high school years—just long enough for me to realize I couldn't keep pushing my foot to the accelerator as I had. Being relentlessly productive was erasing my ability to be present. The sun's rays finally cutting through months of cold gave me a moment to step outside of myself. At that point, I was running a little side decorating business, volunteering for the kids' classrooms in a variety of ways, and teaching spinning classes. I was also substituting at my kids' preschool, choreographing and performing in a fundraising show for the middle school, and training for a half-marathon. This was what stay-at-home moms in the suburbs were doing, and it never dawned on me to not be so busy. I enjoyed these outlets but didn't realize the ways in which they depleted me and tamped down my frustrations rather than giving me respite from them. I gave myself no time to check in to determine how anxious I was feeling, let alone to pause and reflect on what I needed.

After Chris's summer drinking incident, I parented him with extra hypervigilance. I was in complete survival mode. Freedom and friends were his only desires, and those two things conflicted with my attempts to provide some structure and have him around. When he was home, he put an emotional wall up. He was angry with me for trying to keep the bee from its honey. I recalled how hard it had been for him to share me with his sister and brother when he was little. Now he acted like he didn't want any of my attention, but I knew he needed it. I also knew he needed more discipline, and I continued to be uncomfortable with that because I was trying to avoid every one of our interactions becoming a battle.

One night the kids were all strewn across the couch in the family room watching TV.

"Mom," William asked, "what is Scooby Doo doing? Is this going to be scary? What happens next?"

Chris, who had climbed onto the top of the couch, looked down at his little brother from his perch and rolled his eyes.

I reached over from my chair, placed my hand on William's shoulder, and whispered, "Sweetie, Scooby-Doo is chasing the ghost. It's going to be okay. We just have to watch quietly." Chris was easily overstimulated, which made him irritable. William, at age seven, could be over-stimulating.

"Mom, can I have some more popcorn?" William asked.

"Shhhh, just a minute, Sugar." I gave Will a look of warning because I hated it when Chris took it out on his brother and sister. But to no avail. I caught Caroline's eye, and it was clear we both knew what was coming.

"Mom, I need some more popcorn. And can I have butter on it?" William spoke louder this time.

"William, you need to shut up. We're watching a show!" Chris kicked his foot in Will's direction.

"I want some more popcorn. Moooommm!" William droned.

"Okay, I'll make some more. Can you try not to interrupt?" I'm back in familiar territory, trying to step around landmines like I did with my dad. Doing whatever I can not to make Chris mad, hoping William will quiet down as soon as I can get him his popcorn, all while dreading the inevitable.

I wasn't even to the kitchen when I heard William cry out, "Mom, he hit me! Mom, he's hitting me!"

I ran back into the family room, where Chris was holding Caroline off with one hand while he punched William in the shoulder with the other. I yanked William away, yelled at Chris to go up to his room, and agonized over my inability to stop us from being trapped in a painful loop. I wondered what I could do differently and asked myself where my sweet boy had gone. He was more often irritable and restless than not, and I wasn't sure if this was adolescence exacerbating his behavior or if there was more to it.

Later that summer, Joe walked in from work around ten on a Friday night, and I raced to greet him. My nerves were often frayed by the time he got home. I always hoped he could get through to Chris when I could not. Unfortunately, there was usually some yelling involved, but at least I wasn't the one doing it. Thankfully, Joe didn't become enraged the way my father had when I was growing up. Anger, including my own, scared me.

I was still wrapping my mind around my boy's impetuous behavior, but nothing was working. My new plan was to get Joe and I on the same page. Usually one of us would give in because of exhaustion or because we didn't want him to be mad at us. I'd learned from my parenting books about the importance of presenting a unified front to prevent triangulation.

Chris was so powerful in his ability to impact the rest of us. Like my dad, he could change the energy in our home. I cultivated a sixth sense for assessing my dad's mood the second he walked in the door after work. However, I never knew what to expect from him, especially when he was drinking. My son's behavior was becoming just as unpredictable.

"Hi, honey!" I began as soon as I reached Joe. "Chris is talking about sleeping over at a friend's tonight. I'm trying to have him spend the night out only once a weekend. Really, it should be like once a month, if at all, because we have no idea what he's up to." I said this knowing Joe wouldn't be around to enforce it and wouldn't want to because we both just wanted our son to be happy. I also knew Chris simply couldn't be kept from his friends, but I was becoming desperate.

"You're right. I'll talk to him," Joe replied wearily.

"I'm happy to be there, too, because I think we should reinforce this together."

"I've got it," Joe assured me. "I don't want to overwhelm him with both of us talking at him. Then he'll just fight it." Joe trudged off toward the bedroom to change clothes.

I deferred but felt ineffectual and alone. While it was true that Joe was better able to get Chris to comply, I wanted to have control over how things were presented too.

Joe attempted to handle it as he'd promised, but the following week Chris was off at another sleepover. We lacked leverage and credibility, so Chris simply did what he wanted no matter how we tried to reason with him or use consequences and punishments.

Since Chris's first foray into drinking had resulted in a friend becoming unconscious, I became driven to prevent him from any risk of addiction. Already so incapable of considering consequences, the power of his genes became undeniable. Up until then, I had been naively counting on nurture to offset nature. Chris was slated to go to the local public high school in the fall. He'd been to football camp at a military school about an hour away in Wisconsin the summer before and enjoyed it so much that he wanted to go back again this summer. That's when I began to think about the possibility of sending him to high school there. I thought maybe the rules and discipline of a highly structured program might help him learn to do as he was told.

When I mentioned the idea to Joe and reminded him of my concern that Chris seemed susceptible to developing a problem with alcohol, he wasn't convinced. "We've given him a loving home and everything he could ask for. Just because Chris likes his freedom and doesn't listen doesn't mean he's going to have a problem," he said.

"But honey, I'm scared," I admitted. "Kids with ADD are more likely to have addiction issues." I paused, trying to relax but feeling like we couldn't risk more experimentation with alcohol that could lead to his inheriting the disease. "And you know Chris. He's always going to do what his friends are doing, and I'm pretty sure I know what they are doing. He's so impulsive. He's reckless. If we try sending him to St. John's—"

"No way, Sal. Sending him to military school is blowing this all out of proportion. I don't want to send him away!"

"Well, neither do I, but the Whites sent James there, and he really likes it," I say, referring to our neighbors down the street. "Maybe we should talk to them and find out what it's like—"

"It's probably really expensive, and he'd hate it." Joe cut me off again. He shook his head and scowled. I knew he blamed me for not being better able to rein in Chris, and I knew he wasn't worried the way I was.

But I needed Joe to understand how strongly I felt about getting Chris more help. As the oldest child and the child of an alcoholic, I'd felt responsible for my brothers' well-being. Now the responsibility of caring for my children weighed heavily on me. I felt pressure to fix things for my children.

"The structure at St. John's would be good for Chris," I insisted. "If he's forced to go to classes, he'll see he's smarter than he thinks he is. I want him to feel more confident in school and enjoy learning. I don't know what to do, honey. He's really tough on Caroline and William. I can't think of what else . . ." My voice trailed off. The more I thought about it, the more I knew it was time to wave a white flag and finally admit I couldn't manage Chris's behavior.

Joe and I would get caught up in our responsibilities—his at work, mine at home—and then Chris would end up causing enough trouble that Joe and I would have another conversation, still resulting in not knowing what to do. Unfortunately, neither of us had been able to make a difference. Joe's work hours at the dealership, always long, had ramped up even more during the recession, and Caroline and William's activities required more and more of my time and energy. Eventually, at a loss, Joe begrudgingly agreed we should try sending him to St. John's. I hadn't been able to come up with an alternative plan. All I could do was hope this would provide a safe place to build Chris's confidence and steer him away from further experimentation.

thirteen

ummer is in full force with a bright azure Christopher sky. As I lean back in the lounge chair on the deck, I close my eyes and absorb the warmth of the sun's rays. Joe's book-in-progress is a collection of all the writing he's been doing in the middle of the night. He reports being awakened by Chris and drawn into his office, where he listens to the messages Chris gives him and writes them down. When he reads his "downloads" to me from Christopher, I can't help wondering if what he writes is simply what he is hoping to hear. I want it to be true. They sound like him. Joe explains that Chris talks to him by placing thoughts in his mind that Chris wants him to share with other grieving parents, reassuring us that our children are still with us in spirit.

My communication with Chris is very different. I wish I could hear him or see him, but I do feel him. I sense his presence in my heart. Maybe it's wishful thinking, but when the sun shines on my face, it's like he's here. I sit quietly, listening to the cars cruise past our yard and the windchimes stir in the breeze. My concept of time has been skewed since Chris died. I have heard that grief can affect memory. Recently, someone asked what I'd done for my fiftieth birthday, and I got it mixed up with my fortieth. It's crazy how time itself feels different to me, much harder to pin down. It seems to slow like syrup and then pick up so rapidly that I lose my bearings and can't keep pace. I don't want to keep up. Especially since time's passing takes Chris further from me.

I survey our yard from our wooden deck where so many memories collect. I hear a slight breeze move through the leaves of the walnut tree overhead and indulge myself in memories of Christopher in this very spot. I played with him here in the orange inflatable baby pool, looking up at the airplanes sailing past. My little boy joyfully running through the sprinkler, flying along the rings of the swing set we long ago took down. The forsythia bushes have already bloomed bright yellow and since faded along our fence. I feel him as close as the sunlight shimmering in waves. I try to absorb his light. As I let it wash over me, I sink deeper into the lounge chair, flipping through my memories like slides clicking in a projector. They begin with his birthday parties as a child and continue through his teenage years, zooming in on our outdoor family dinners at the round garden table after the sun sets and the fireflies appear. Opening my eyes, I can almost see my boy racing up the deck stairs in the boots he'd carelessly toss to the floor as he opens the sliding glass door to the kitchen. I begin to hear the Rolling Stone's "Wild Horses" in my head. Is it God's way of reminding me nothing can keep me from him? That we'll meet again in Heaven? There we'll be someday after I die, the two of us riding horses side by side along the beach, the sea spray splashing between us as we run free.

A wild horse has become one of my signs for him. I need these signs to know he's around. They become a lifeline. I text him in my journal entries, and since I'm constantly crying, I'm becoming acquainted with the sound of my own cry in my ears. *Where are you?* I keep asking as the breeze picks up. I look out over the fence to the street, where I happen to catch the silver emblem flashing on a black Mustang convertible as it flies past. Coincidence? It helps me hold on.

My wild horse couldn't be tamed. From the start he didn't want to be tied down. When I'd buckle him into his car seat as a little boy, he'd arch his back, not having it. Within minutes after our first preschool drop-off, he fell. Blood gushed out near his eye. The teachers said it happened so fast that no one had seen it. I scooped him up in my arms, raced down the street to my car, and off to the emergency room we went. The doctors had to wrangle him into a little white papoose to give him stitches. I'm not sure which of us was more tortured.

I've made it to the mountains of Montana for the writing retreat. Just yesterday I grabbed Christopher's prayer card and a soft, green, swirly rock he gave me and tucked them into a little pouch in my carry-on. It is getting increasingly harder to leave the comfort of home (I think because it feels like I am leaving Christopher), so I had to talk myself into the Uber to get to the airport in time for my flight. Before I leave my room for breakfast, I pull my prayer card out and study my son's face, staring deeply into his eyes and asking him to help me touch back into the reassurance that everything is going to be all right.

On the third day of the retreat, feeling nestled in the coziness of a community of women with stories to tell, I become more committed to writing my book. Yearning for Christopher, I'm needing direction, a means to connect to him so deeply that our souls touch. Listening to the other women who've come to learn about the craft of writing, I am inspired. Walking arm-in-arm with new friends under the stars, I make a vow to see it through.

The following day I am surprised to discover that I'm the only one in our group who signed up for an equine therapy session at a nearby ranch. I find myself seated next to a small, weathered woman in her pickup truck. I'm intentionally stepping out of my comfort zone and seizing the moment like never before. Maybe Chris is guiding me to live life the way he did by taking a big bite out of it.

I study the rancher's strong hands on the steering wheel, admiring the turquoise rings she has on every finger. She tells me right away that she usually likes to spend the drive sharing her story. I nestle into my seat for what I'm pretty sure will be a story of hardship. There is something both tough and gentle about this woman.

As we bump along an empty dirt road, she begins. "I have had some challenges in my life that led me to where I am now. I never would have guessed I'd become an equine therapist, but here I am." She tells me about her abusive childhood that paved the way for her to end up in an abusive marriage. "I became addicted to alcohol, and I became suicidal," she shares, "and somehow was fortunate enough to enter a program of recovery many years ago, which changed my life."

Bobbi tells me more—about her daughter, Cedar, who was born with Down's Syndrome, about her breast cancer diagnosis, and how, during surgery to remove the tumor, her heart stopped. I study her more closely, her piercing eyes focused on the road ahead when she says, "All I can tell you is that when my heart stopped, I felt myself being transported way above my body toward a huge pool of light. I became a part of this bigger pool of light, separate but connected with other individual bright lights." She slows down, pulls into her ranch, and faces me, still reliving what that was like.

"Really?" I interrupt. "I . . . I . . . lost my son Christopher five months ago, and it would be amazing if he had an experience like that. . . ." I trail off imagining it.

She nods as if she already knows about my loss, but still wrapped up in her story, she goes on. "I didn't want to leave that state of pure bliss, but I heard a voice tell me my work on earth wasn't done and that I had to go back. The voice told me I needed to return to help heal other people." She pulls the keys out of the ignition and, as we both step down from the truck, concludes her story. "I have been healthy ever since. I went back to school to study equine therapy, and I've been able to carry out my life's work right here on my ranch."

She leads me through a small tack room out to a field filled with horses. As we approach them, I envision what she described, picturing souls rising toward a circle of light joined by other individual soul's lights collecting to become one. Bobbi's story helps me have faith that "the other side" that Joe so fiercely believes in can be something I can believe in too. My intuition is raising its voice. I've been given reassurance that Christopher is being held in the light and that there may be a divine plan after all. Look at what Bobbi had to endure to find purpose and meaning in her life.

We stand side-by-side, overlooking the horses in the field. I take in the Appaloosas and Bays and the black and chestnut horses, whose colors begin to wash together as the rain starts to fall. Bobbi points to her daughter Cedar, who is leading horses from the barn in her rain boots, completely unbothered by the downpour now falling from the vast Montana sky.

I watch as Bobbi walks straight toward a beautiful black horse, tall and muscular, with a sheen on its back. She tells me that she is guided to which of her horses to pick for each session. Once inside, I'm given a felt hard hat in black, just like the ones I used to wear at summer camp. I can hear Cedar singing, so I peek outside to watch her jumping around in puddles. The sheets of rain stream off the roof. Bobbi calls me over. She hitches my horse, Bugle, to a post and begins to brush him out. I can't take my eyes off him. He holds his head high and his long mane flows down his neck. When I approach him with my hand thrust toward his shoulder, he backs away and turns his head off to the side. Bobbi suggests I wait to touch him and instructs me to follow his lead and mirror his actions.

"Equine therapy is an intuitive process. I don't necessarily have a plan other than to guide you along and trust my gut as I observe your interaction with him," she tells me.

She unhitches Bugle, and he heads to the outside of the ring, black mane shining. I go over to stand next to him, wanting to lay my head along his long neck. He begins to walk around the ring, and I walk alongside him. As we walk, and I attempt to keep up with him, Bobbi suggests, "Talk to him as if he's your son. Tell him what you want your son to hear. But stay in your body and keep breathing."

I'm nervous, which isn't how I usually feel around horses. But I'll try anything to connect with my son. I try to steady myself and self-consciously whisper, "Hi, Sweetheart. Momma is here. Momma loves you. Can you feel it? Are you there?" I know Bugle isn't Christopher, but at the same time I so long for a tangible target for my affection, for something I can see and touch to believe his spirit is near. Bugle turns his gorgeous head away from me and continues to walk around the outside of the ring. I force my arm to remain down at my side to give him a wide berth even though I want to nuzzle up against him. It's hard not to reach for him as I keep up with his quickening pace. Bobbi encourages me to continue to talk to him. "Hi, darlin'. Momma wants to be close to you." I hear my desperation and see myself from Bobbi's point of view. I am enamored of this big, stand-offish, wild animal and just want to get closer to him. I also appreciate that there is something about this chase that feels strikingly familiar.

The chase around the ring continues, and I observe myself clumsily trying to keep up with him, giving him his space but wanting him to let me get closer. Amid this well-worn dance, I begin to ask myself what I'm doing. Why am I working so hard to connect when it only creates more distance? What is it I want back? I suppose I need to know my love matters. That I matter. To think of myself as a good mom, I need to do something, be a mom who bathes her son in love. There is a risk of suffocating him in this love, but I never want him to question its presence as I had to with my father. I need to know that all the love pouring out of me for him will reach its destination.

Tears fall as I maintain my focus on one of Bugle's big dark eyes and its lashes and start to digest the meaning of what is happening. Tension slides off my shoulders as we enter a syncopated dance. In this trance-like state, I have an awakening. I see how hard I tend to push. I realize my yearnings began long before Chris was born. Even before he died, I sought connection with him instead of trusting in the connection that was already there. I couldn't just let it be. I think of Chris's tweet, "Life is honestly so beautiful, as long as you allow it to be," and suddenly, I understand. When I was a little girl, I must have concluded I wasn't good enough for my dad to love since I couldn't feel it. I thought I had to go after his love, work at it, chase it. I've always had trouble trusting that love can be unconditional. Love simply is. I don't have to keep trying to earn it. This is one of Christopher's greatest teachings for me. To embrace the beautiful gift of being his mom and cherish all the love that exists between us.

Our children are meant to be given the roots of unconditional love without demand. My connection with Chris is profound. I trust that Chris's spirit has wings divinely set in motion. I would never want to hold him back. I see how, after Christopher died, I fell back into the chase. Without knowing where his spirit was, I pushed to feel him again. Now it's time to have faith that he can be both by my side and soaring somewhere. Here with Bugle, I let everything else slip away. I let go and trust. Bugle no longer turns away or appears disinterested. I relish the new energy and flow between us and feel lighter with each step. I feel connected to him in motion. It dawns on me that as I let him set the pace, it helps him feel at ease. Without fear driving our interaction, we are free just to be. As Bobbi slows him down, I feel secure even after Bugle ventures from my side. He walks away, and as he does, I understand that to truly love means to let go of my own agenda and accept what is. I believe that acceptance will be an essential part of my grieving and will lessen my suffering.

Back home after the retreat, I try to bolster myself for work on Monday. Instead of feeling uplifted as I did while I was engaged in learning about writing, I am tired out from the travel, and when I'm tired, my grief takes on more intensity and becomes overwhelming. I return to the past and weigh my decisions. My heart was so soft when it came to Christopher. I don't think it was easy to be him, but it was easy to love him, even when I didn't always know what to do with him.

My heart felt especially soft when we dropped Chris off at the military academy in late August for his freshman year of high school. I looked at my beautiful boy with his fresh brush cut and wondered, *Who sends her child away? What am I doing?*

Chris wouldn't look at me as I made up his bed with fresh

white sheets and a blanket. I tried to pretend he was back at sleepaway camp and wouldn't be gone for long. I tried to think of the old stone hall of dorm rooms as a safe shelter while ignoring the ache in my chest. Sweat trickled down my forehead. I turned on the fan next to his bed.

"Dad and I will come up next week for your first football game," I told Chris, who was standing sullenly in the middle of the room, his eyes on the floor. "We'll come up for as many games as we can, so it won't be long til we see you, okay?"

Joe sat silently on the bed across from Chris's. I felt the blame he was harboring against me because this had been my idea. He'd miss having Chris around. The three of us walked from Chris's dorm across the campus, and I tried hard to maintain my conviction that the school would be a place to reset for Christopher, where his self-esteem would grow and the routine would bring security. He could play football, begin to enjoy schoolwork, and avoid getting into the trouble alcohol and drugs could bring.

As we passed boys in their uniforms, I tried to look beneath their military caps into their eyes and determine if they were happy. St. John's touted itself as a character-building all-boys college prep whose cadets discovered their strengths and developed the confidence to succeed academically and in leadership positions.

Although it was a sunny day, the tall pine trees loomed overhead, and I felt a chill. We took an obligatory picture sitting on an imposing stone wall in the shadows. I steeled myself not to cry as I hugged my son goodbye and made a commitment to myself that I would always do the right things for my children, even if they were hard. I would sacrifice having him home if it meant I'd get to see a smile return to his face. I'd do anything to see him feel proud of himself.

fourteen

*H*ere it is the middle of July, the first summer without Christopher alive, and I'm back at work. The team here is amazingly supportive, which comes as no surprise. I'm among colleagues who work hard to help patients get clean and sober and improve their lives, but I'm unsettled. I forgot how much floating between different positions in my resource role keeps me on my toes. I'm filling in for case managers, stepping in to do assessments, and the team is hoping I can teach some seminars for my friend Ina, who's just been diagnosed with stage four cancer and is taking some time off. If it hadn't been for Ina, I wouldn't have gotten this job. I'd do anything for her.

Right after Chris headed to college, I renewed my lapsed social work license and started to earn hours toward my clinical license. My plan is to ultimately start the private therapy practice I intended to open years ago before baby Christopher arrived. I briefly entertained returning to work in a more creative capacity, but let's face it, being a therapist with a specialty in addiction is a natural fit. The year and a half I've worked in the field so far has convinced me this is my calling, despite fighting it. I know it's the work Chris wants me to do. I need to feel like my life has purpose and meaning, and I hope he's proud of me.

A few weeks in, I'm getting into the groove. Just like every day since I started, I collapse into my car at the end of the day, re-remembering I've lost my son and feeling overwhelmed by the grief I've kept at bay while working. I'm overtaken by it. My heart can't hold all the emotion, and it all comes spilling out as I crumple over my steering wheel in tears. How can someone so full of life not be here living? Where should I put the love for him that pours out with my pain?

On the drive home I ask myself why all the missing I did when Chris was alive didn't better prepare me for the missing I'm doing now. I think about what it was like after dropping Chris at St. John's. In no time, it became clear that most of the boys who went there were also non-compliant kids with ADD and learning issues. Somehow that hadn't occurred to me before. When we went up to watch him play football, we'd get a glimpse of his green eyes beneath his helmet as he caught the ball and ran. I got the feeling he would keep running beyond the field as far as he could if not for the game. I cheered from the sidelines, but my cheers fell flat.

When we drove up to see Chris for one of the military award ceremonies, he wasn't beaming with pride as I'd hoped. He appeared instead as if he were back in the hospital in the straitjacket-like papoose they put him in when he was small and needed stitches. He looked gorgeous, marching past in his uniform and eyes straight ahead, but he did not love the school the way our neighbor's son had. I started to question what I'd been thinking, and whatever hope I'd had that this would make things better began to disappear.

As I took in his lean figure standing out from the rest, I felt the fullness of how much I missed him. I wondered how we'd gotten here. I just wanted to break into the formation of young men and hug my boy. It was so hard to have him away. But, at the same time, I experienced some comfort in knowing he was being looked after better than I could. I also experienced an undercurrent of guilt for being relieved that my nervous system could take a bit of a breather. And with him away, to be able to show up for Caroline and William. Caroline, who'd been able to take care of herself in a way that her brothers could not, had gotten a bit lost in the shuffle. She was settling in well to the new private Catholic school she had transferred to from public school. At eleven, she had taken the initiative to facilitate the transition. I made it my goal to show up for her more than ever.

That fall, I didn't miss a single one of her basketball or volleyball games. She didn't especially like athletics, but she was making new friends and had become a cheerleader for her new school's football team. I dragged myself to go watch her cheer while Joe was at work. Feeling low and missing my boy, I tried to get to know Caroline's new friends' moms, but they spent time on the sidelines talking about healthy meals they were cooking while I felt like I was an alien who'd landed on a foreign white picket fence planet. In my mind, I'm an outsider. I've concluded that every other mother is "normal," easily able to care for their children, and carefree, while I am worried. But these women have known each other for a long time. It's like they all took a vote and agreed they must be overprotective and hover extra close to their children, just as I was having to let go. I thought about Christopher in his faraway dorm room in that huge stone building. He's at military school, for God's sake. How did this happen? And then I looked back at the moms as they chatted, feeling the stark divide between me and them.

I took Caroline shopping for dresses for her weekly school dances, but my timing was off. Just as I was attempting to be more present in her life, she was relishing her independence and feeling more secure than she had at public school. It didn't seem to matter to her whether I was there for her or not, but I was committed to showing up anyway.

I volunteered more, too, supervising in William's elementary school lunchroom and helping in the art room and library so I could see him during the school day. Despite being very involved with William and trying to be more available for Caroline, sending Chris away felt like an indictment of my failure as a mother. Behind my smile, I felt removed from the other mothers. I was preoccupied with missing him, just as I'd previously been preoccupied with worry.

In mid-November of that fall of Chris's freshman year, Joe and I got a call from St. John's informing us that a bunch of boys, including Chris, had snuck off-campus. I was crestfallen. Military school was backfiring. Not only had the boys left a campus that was supposed to be secure, complete with a gated entrance, but they headed straight to the local grocery store and promptly got caught trying to steal liquor. As I took in the story, my fantasy of keeping Chris safe and sober began to shatter. I had a familiar sensation of falling infinitely backward into space. The school reassured us this wouldn't happen again, but my confidence was shaken.

Before long, it was winter break. Joe went to pick Chris up while I stayed home with Caroline and William. Waiting for Chris at the door when they pulled into the garage, I called out, "Babe, I'm so glad you're home. I want to hear everything!" I hoped my enthusiasm to have him home covered up my lack of enthusiasm for his school. I was glad to have him where I could see him and desperate to get more information than I'd been able to pull out of him during our phone calls. I hugged Chris tightly. I'd missed him so much more than I'd imagined was possible, but he was already on the move.

"Yeah, Mom. There's nothing to tell. It's not great. I'm going

out tonight, okay?" He threw down his duffle and headed upstairs toward the shower. Joe nodded my way, insinuating I
should let him be.

"I know your friends want to see you, but before you head
out, I just want to get more of a sense of whether things have
been going any better. How are your classes? Is taking your medication every day helping you enjoy learning at all?" I asked as I
followed him up the stairs and down the hall.

"Honestly, Mom, like I've said, everybody there takes meds.
Some of the guys store theirs up and sell them to other guys.
And, uh, we just end up copying off each other, so no, I'm not
learning anything much." He headed to the bathroom as I stood
speechless, knowing he was trying to shock me and not sure
what to believe.

Before Chris shut the door behind him, he took off his shirt
and I caught a glimpse of his angular chest, tapering down to his
slim waist. I also caught a glimpse of what looked like several
raised red wounds, two on his chest and one on his shoulder.

"Oh my God, babe, what happened? What are those marks?"
I moved over to him and gently laid my fingers where his skin
was scarred and angry. I felt faint, and the room spun.

My beautiful boy looked back at me. "Momma, let me take a
shower, and I'll tell you about it later," he promised. "I gotta be at
Justin's at five. Their break just started too."

The next day Joe and I approached the big armchair Chris was
tucked inside in the family room. He sat playing a video game
with a Gatorade in his lap, his legs outstretched.

"Precious, can you pause the game for a sec?" I asked gently.

"What's up?" His head popped out, and I spotted the remote
control dangling from his wrist.

"Dad and I just want to know how you got those burn marks. Where did they come from?"

Joe chimed in, "Chris, what happened? I gotta get to work, but Mom told me I needed to see your chest."

"Moooommmmm. Come on!" Chris looked up at us, knowing he couldn't avoid the conversation. "There's this gang at St. John's called El Presidente," he began as he grabbed his T-shirt and pulled it over his head. "They're a bunch of older guys. One day they came into my room and jumped me."

"What?" roared Joe. "Slow down, buddy, and tell us what they did." Joe took a closer look at the red welts on Chris's otherwise unblemished chest. He turned to me as he studied one of the half-moon-shaped scars, "Sal, it's not that bad."

Chris grabbed his shirt and slipped his arms through the sleeves, "Look guys. I told you St. John's isn't what you think it is. These guys showed up in my room, jumped me, shoved me onto the ground, and branded me."

"Oh, sweetheart, I'm so sorry this happened to you." Tears sprang from my eyes. As if I'd been there, I viscerally experienced my son lying on the hard floor of his dorm room with a gang of boys standing above him, victimizing my baby. Chris seemed even more distracted than usual, not looking me in the eye, but I couldn't assess what he was feeling. I was too frightened and angry on his behalf as each of his wounds felt burned into my own flesh. No one had protected him. And I was the one who had put him in harm's way.

He looked up at us briefly before starting his game back up, but I couldn't detect any emotion. I assumed he was trying to be tough about it. Joe walked up the stairs and I followed behind him, mortified. I couldn't stop imagining those boys taking a lighter to Christopher's body and branding him. I'd failed my son. I would never be able to forgive myself. The letdown I felt in the school paled in comparison to the shame that seeped out of my pores.

A week later, Chris was sitting on the striped couch in the basement when Joe returned from his appointment with the president of St. John's to discuss the incident. Chris didn't want to go back, and we didn't want him to either.

"How'd it go?" Chris asked nonchalantly when Joe and I walked downstairs.

I was anxious to hear all about it, too, since by then we'd decided that Chris would not be returning. We also wanted our money back.

Joe stood between Chris and his video game to ensure Chris was paying attention. "I showed up ready to slay a dragon," Joe began. "I expected Danishes and coffee on a wheeled serving cart. I stood waiting for my apology and a check. Instead, the president told me they had taken our accusations very seriously. They investigated our claims, and . . ." Joe paused for effect as he stepped over to lean against the wall, "they told me they don't have any gangs called the El Presidentes. They do, however, have a group of honor students whose parents are prestigious Mexican high-ranking military, political, and diplomatic members." Joe looked down at Chris with an expression that appeared to me to be pride instead of the anger and frustration I anticipated because our son had clearly lied. He shook his head. "We aren't getting our money back for next semester, and I've got to hand it to you, Chris. I've told you some of my stories from when I was young and crazy, but you beat me with this one. Good riddance to that place, buddy."

He patted Chris on the back and turned to me. "Sal, get him enrolled at New Trier, and let's put the whole thing behind us."

Joe headed up to the kitchen, shaking his head. A small smile of bemused admiration played over his features.

I, on the other hand, was reeling as I tried to process the fact that Chris's story had been a lie. Joe later elaborated on what really happened. A bunch of the cadets voluntarily competed in a crazy game to see how long they could withstand a searing hot penny pressed against their skin. All of this was revealed by the school's investigation.

Joe hadn't been in favor of sending Chris to military school in the first place. I could see how strongly he identified with Chris. His insistence on moving forward felt like an "I told you so." I'd driven the decision and it had failed. My husband's willingness to let the whole thing go made me question my perception of reality. Was I overreacting?

I felt betrayed by Chris. It was baffling to me that he could lie so blatantly and convincingly. It made me think of my dad, who I'd had to steel myself to confront about his drinking, only to have him deny the truth to my face. Once, when he pulled up onto the curb outside our house for my daughter's birthday party, I asked him if he was drunk. "Absolutely not!" he insisted as he unsteadily sauntered toward the party.

Chris's face lit up with relief when Joe left the room. I wanted to feel relieved, too, but I was still stranded back in that horrific place where what Chris had told us was true. I grew up with three younger brothers and two younger stepbrothers, so I understood boys. A little piece of me admired the ingenuity it took for Chris to create such a dramatic story, but I didn't think I'd be able to shake the images embedded in my psyche of my child being pinned down and tortured.

A mix of familiar feelings swirled inside me. A post-traumatic response of helplessness, guilt, and isolation left me too stupefied to do anything other than to make sure Chris knew that lying was not okay and to plead with him for things to be different now that he was back home. When I told him there would be rules to follow, he insisted he would, and I wanted to believe him.

I was glad to have him home, but I also knew what was in store. I didn't have the slightest notion of how I was going to handle my boy back at the large public high school and entering a developmental stage where it was appropriate to grant him more of the independence he insisted upon. The weight of my job as his mother felt heavy.

fifteen

*I*t is July 28. Marcia's birthday. Marcia is Joe's sister and Chris's godmother, and we are wondering if this will be her last birthday with us. She's had such a long journey battling cancer, persistently undergoing surgeries, chemotherapy, and radiation treatments. Once so hearty, she persists with such resilience. An inspiration, as even with her walker in hand and on a hefty regimen of pain medication, she is a ray of sunshine. After losing Christopher, Joe and I try to prepare ourselves for losing another one of our favorite humans. I wish I could have spared her from bearing witness to our pain and her own when Chris died. The McQuillen family has suffered so much loss. Marcia and Joe have also lost a niece, a brother, and a sister in the last three years.

Marcia is the big sister I never had. I once confessed to her, around the time Chris was entering adolescence, how hard it was to parent him. "He never does anything I tell him to do," I complained. "I've never seen anything like it. It's so hard, and Joey is never home." This was during a trip to her home in Florida. We sat out by her pool under the lanai, stealing a moment before Joe came back with the kids. I felt disloyal, but Marcia is one of the most compassionate people I've ever met. I knew she'd bathe me in sympathy.

She pulled her chair closer. "My sweet Christopher. Isn't he something?" She giggled. "Remember when I took him for a ride in the convertible when he was two? I have a video I've got to show you." Of course she did. She took photos and videos throughout our visits when we'd descend upon her and Tom with our little ones each spring. It started to dawn on me that she raised her own children single-handedly and watched her dad work long hours while her mom raised ten children. She was unfazed by my distress. Suddenly I realized I had just been complaining to her about all she'd ever known. After all, she grew up with five brothers, including Joe, who had surely been a lot like my boy.

Marcia encouraged me to come inside so she could show me the video. As she played it, it was clear she was so enamored by Christopher that she couldn't entertain the possibility that he was difficult. She was focused only on the joy he brought. Looking at the video, I watched the sunny freshness of my son's sparkly eyes reflected in my sister-in-law's twinkling ones. Her loyalty to him was reciprocated. She prompted him to sing "Zip-a-Dee-Doodah," and he didn't hesitate. Where was his defiance then? I heard her sweet voice encouraging him as she recorded my two-year-old, buckled into his car seat, little brown legs not reaching the floor. They sang off-key, and it was the sweetest thing I'd ever seen. I saw how he stole his aunt's heart from the beginning and how she stole his. His pure innocence garnered her delight and applause.

Later that afternoon of Marcia's birthday, I find myself at Christopher's grave as I often do. I tend to it since I can't tend to him. I am forming a ritual, placing the heart-shaped rocks I've gathered, setting other memorabilia along the edges of his gravestone that friends have left here: the Buffalo Bills golf ball, guitar pic, miniature Cubs chair. I wipe it clean, setting each item in place, dig up some weeds, and rub my hand slowly across the letters carved in the stone. Today the letters are warm from the sun, and I imagine it is Christopher's skin I'm touching. I sit down in the grass, reflecting on all the loss.

I picture the corner table where the oldest generation of McQuillens sits every August in Canada at our annual Club dinner. That table is emptying, a new generation filling in. Will Marcia be able to join us this year? I anticipate a changing of the guard. Another ring of our family tree is forming, and I wonder how it's possible that life can still move forward when my son isn't here.

I look out beyond the cemetery to the big tree in the distance and think about how Chris is motivating me to be strong like a tree, like the necklace he gave me. I know there is a deep-down part of me that is all right, or at least knows someday I will be. Holding my Tree of Life necklace in my hand, I want to find strength. I pull out my phone and look up the word sap. It is the fluid that circulates inside the tree, distributing water and nutrients. Chris is becoming my sap. He is my fuel. He will give me the strength I need to handle all the loss in the air. Consumed with losing Chris, I know I am bracing against any more of it. The prospect of more loss pulls feelings from inside me, like a comb being dragged through my hair, yanking from my roots the loss of my son.

I continue to rub my hands along the letters of Christopher's name. I shake my head and utter "NOOOO," as I do every time the truth sets in. *My son is dead.* Most days I'm here, I imagine him walking out from behind the trees—not really lying underground. It's my nightmare in the flesh. The pity I rarely grant myself overcomes me. I can't hear his low, stuttering voice, a mix of boy and man. I can't have his enthusiasm sputter forth into the tangled words I'd ask him to repeat. I don't get to look adoringly at the Indian-red, clay-pot color of his tanned skin. I can't giggle under my breath, getting such a kick out of the way he absorbed and repeated sayings like, "You're the bee's knees, Mom." Or steal a look as he took several stairs at a time, flew toward the door after a shower, and hummed under his breath as he got ready. I can't take pleasure in his contentment, even knowing he was happiest when he was heading out.

And that face. I'll never forget his Ashton Kutcher impersonation, his hand encircling his face with his sideways grin. "This is the money-maker. I know that." Oh, that gorgeous face. Thin neck, generous bottom lip, buzz cut with a cowlick, red-tinted scruff on his chin. His beautiful eyes, gazing off to the next place he'd rather be. I miss the warmth radiating out from under his palm resting on my shoulder just long enough to feel his affection.

God, I miss the trouble, my "rebel without a pause." The heart-beating urgency of his latest mishap. Even the drama and frustration of powerlessness when it came to slowing him down and having any influence over him to take better care of himself. Eat something, get more rest, brush his teeth. I miss the cherished interruptions that provided me with my soul's delight—the chance to reassure and comfort him. I'd stare into that captivating face of his and give in to his charm, rub his back. And rather than hold on tight and never let him go, I always watched as he walked away.

I kneel and lower my legs out beneath me, my stomach touching the grass. I lie down, my forehead touching Christopher's gravestone. Then I turn my head as if I can rest it against his shoulder. I stay only for a moment before I stand up to make sure I'm still alone, shake off the ache I can still taste, and find my way back through other gravestones to my car.

During the year-and-a-half after his return home from military school, any bit of compliance he'd had when he first returned quickly unraveled. Back in the second semester of freshman year at the public high school, Chris soon threw caution back out the window. Once he knew for sure we weren't going to send him back to military school, he resumed giving me a run. This only contributed to my shame, perpetuated by continuing to combat my anxiousness. I could barely get my kids to their three separate schools compared to other suburban mothers who were so put-together, pulling up to Starbucks before school with flocks of primly dressed children falling out of the car to follow in their paths like little ducks in a row.

By the time Chris started his sophomore year, Joe was still working until at least ten o'clock on Friday nights and twelve hours on Saturdays. I understood Chris's ongoing desire for freedom. I didn't realize how much I needed my own freedom until becoming a mom. In the early days of my marriage, I'd struggled with not wanting to be tied down. Now frantic energy pumped through my body every day at an elevated rate as I continuously attempted to gain control over my beloved son, who was a combustible mix of our genes and his own strong spirit.

On the rare occasion one of his friends would answer my calls, I'd sit up in bed surprised. "Hi, Brian. It's Mrs. McQuillen again. Sorry to bother you, sweetie, but Chris told me he was spending the night with you. Is he there yet?" I knew the call was a replay of the one from the weekend before. I knew I was being annoying and desperate. But by then Chris, at fifteen, was trying to outrun the addiction that had already taken a stronghold. Driven by a dread I couldn't have named, I persisted.

"Hey, Mrs. McQuillen. I think he, uh, went to another party and isn't back here yet. Let me check." I waited endlessly only to be told, "Yeah, he's not here."

"Well, okay. He isn't answering his cell so please have him call me when he gets back." I surmised that Chris had passed out somewhere or worse. There was some small comfort in having gotten ahold of one of his friends who was either covering for him or who, like me, had no idea where he was.

I got a call one afternoon. Chris had been back home from military school for about a year.

"Mrs. McQuillen? Officer Stanwell from the Winnetka Police Department here."

My heart skipped a beat. "Is everything okay?" My voice shook as I tried to stay calm.

"We've got some boys out on the village playfields smoking weed. We're calling their parents to meet us down the street from the Smith's house where we caught them."

"I'll be right there." I hung up, made sure my other kids were accounted for, and flew out the door. As I drove, I thought about Chris's recent arrest. He and a friend had gotten caught smoking weed in the car, which resulted in being sentenced by a peer jury to several months of community service. Chris was getting into more and more serious trouble, and the incidents were happening with more frequency. We had to enforce more impactful consequences before his actions landed him in the kind of trouble that could negatively impact his future.

I drove past Chris's friend's house to the end of the street, where several police cars were parked. It was dusk, and dark, mauve shadows were just beginning to descend on the lawns of the houses nearby. I spotted several parents standing next to an officer as Christopher and three of his friends emerged from the trees with another officer at their side. I watched Chris step out from the crowd to head my way. His sharp cheekbones jutted out from under his hoodie.

"Mom, this is crazy. I wasn't even doing anything," he said. "The guys were smoking, and they got busted for having paraphernalia, but I was just hanging with them. They can't arrest me. Let's go." Normally inclined to follow his lead, I stopped in my tracks instead. The darkening sky matched my mood. Was he telling me the truth, or could he really lie so easily? I felt lost inside.

"Are you saying you were with them but not smoking weed?"

Chris met my eyes and held my gaze. "One hundred percent. I'm not going back to court, and I'm definitely not doing any more community service because I wasn't smoking."

I wasn't sure what to think. I felt frightened but relieved. I walked over to the group, where several parents I didn't know were shaking their heads. I homed in on the officer who looked like he was in charge. "Hi. I'm Mrs. McQuillen. Are you letting my son go?"

The officer nodded. "He denies up and down that he was smoking, and we didn't find any paraphernalia on him, so we have no choice but to let him go."

I turned away from the group of parents, feeling strangely guilty. Oh, how I wanted to believe my child. I always did. Just as I had when a friend of mine told me Chris was selling weed on the school bus not long after he'd gotten home from St. John's. I'd confronted him about it, he'd completely denied it, and I still wasn't sure what was true. I knew he smoked weed by then, which had been unfathomable to me the year before. I wanted to believe Chris even though I couldn't relate to or fathom how easy it was for him to lie. Since I was inclined to take his behavior personally, when he lied, I felt betrayed.

Christopher kept narrowly escaping major consequences. I felt ineffectual and terrified as I anticipated a summer of more of the same. Was it simply a matter of having a nervous system primed for the threat that made me unable to refrain from worry when it came to my firstborn? I'd wait up for him, staring at the glow my bedside lamp was throwing against the wall, unable to stop my mind from imagining worst-case scenarios. I was wiped out. I wanted him to have a wake-up call without anything bad happening, yet I knew that wasn't possible. I just wanted things to be normal but had no idea what that would look like.

sixteen

$\mathcal{U}$nless they're in extreme denial, every parent of a child struggling with addiction experiences the very real fear that their child could die. Once you come to terms with the fact they have a disease, you realize it could kill them. If you yourself have been in recovery and attended meetings, then you've seen firsthand the lives lost to this brutal affliction with every passing year you stay sober. And once you realize you can't prevent your kids from getting the disease, it becomes about making sure they survive it.

In the months before the end of his sophomore year, Chris became visibly depressed. He had just turned sixteen, so I tried to decipher between cause and effect and realized it didn't really matter. I recognized that, like me, Chris also faced dark clouds lurking under the surface of an outgoing exterior. When he was home, he stayed under the covers in his bedroom with the curtains drawn. His enthusiasm for life was usurped by malaise. Whenever I tried to talk to him, he pulled his comforter over his head until I gave up and left the room. Like most of us with the disease of alcoholism, he had been self-medicating. And very quickly his alcohol and drug use had begun to backfire. This heightened my determination to help him get sober.

I encouraged Joe to talk to Chris one night after he hadn't

left his room all day. I stood quietly in the hallway, peeking into the bedroom from around the door, which was cracked open just a little.

Joe stood over Chris's bed. I heard him authoritatively say, "Chris, I've been sober for many years. I didn't just stop drinking because it sounded like a good idea. I had to stop." Then he lowered his voice to a whisper. "You know that I lost two brothers to suicide. Bobby, when I was in college, then Billy a few years after Mom and I got married. Alcoholism and depression often go hand in hand. I need to know that you're okay. Mommy and I want you to be okay."

As I stood in the hallway, I prayed Joe would be able to get through to him. Much later, Joe joined me downstairs. His face was ashen as he informed me that Chris had been having dark thoughts.

"His depression is bad, Sal. It reminds me of how I felt at the end of my drinking when I didn't want to live like that anymore. I told him about my brothers."

"Wait, Joe. Is he suicidal? Is that what you're telling me?" I did not want to entertain the possibility. I remembered how Marcia had confronted Joe and informed him that she didn't want to lose another brother and how he'd shared that her message had made the necessary impact.

"It's not good. He says he's willing to go somewhere to get clean and sober if it means not feeling so depressed." Joe stood, his tough, take-charge bravado replaced by a vulnerability in his worried eyes. Seeing Chris like this had gotten to him and penetrated in a way that my previous concerns had not. He was now on board to do whatever it would take to save our boy. I felt compassion for my husband and son mixed with an irritation that it had had to get this far.

I soon discovered we'd need to hire an educational consultant to determine the next step. This was an expensive and challenging proposition, especially given our experience with military school. We would need to take another big leap of faith that the consultant and the professionals she'd connect us to would come through. Joe and I each had a tough time relinquishing control over the process because now both of us were afraid.

We found out that most young people are directed first to wilderness programs so they can be removed from their using environments to get clean. We checked out different options and agreed to send Chris to a program in the mountains of Utah, which started on May 15 before school was even out. This time, it felt like I was tearing him from my loins. I battled with myself but ultimately concluded that relying on outside help was the right thing to do. Doing the "right" thing was part of my upbringing, as well as my spiritual training. I convinced myself that sacrificing time with Christopher in the present was the best decision I could make because it was going to save his life. It would be worth it in the end. I was certain doing what was right would guarantee a positive outcome.

Parents in our social circle were baffled when I shared our plan. No one was sending their children away at that time, at least no one I knew. I was doing it for a second time. *Why can't I control my son?* I asked myself, seeing the same question reflected in their eyes. My desire to be understood has often stood in my way, and here, it prompted me to share more than I felt comfortable sharing. Feeling like I owed other people an explanation for our decision, I began relating what I'd learned about wilderness programs—that these were the only options I'd found to stop addiction in its tracks at such a young age. I defended my decision because I felt I had no choice. All I could do was vet them well and ultimately trust my boy to their care.

We couldn't prevent Chris from going out his last night home before leaving for the wilderness program. I was concerned he might change his mind. Especially since this was one of the few times he'd agreed to one of our suggestions.

As the night grew later, Joe went in search of Chris and found him holed up in a garage drinking with some of his friends. When Joe brought him home, he reeked of alcohol, but I couldn't get mad about it. He was still on board to go, hoping as I did that this time, he'd be getting the help it took to feel better. He asked me to rub his back as I had done many times before. I was glad I got to lay my hands on him before I had to let him go. As I squeezed his shoulders, I wrestled inside myself, not wanting to send him away again. I felt my resolve disappear. I told myself to get it together. This was a matter of life or death. My hands grew tired, but I kept rubbing his back, trying to trust that this program would be able to do for him what I could not and get him clean and sober. I wanted to be the one who could make it all better. Wasn't that my job as his mother?

The next morning, while Joe drove Chris to the airport to fly with him to Salt Lake City, I felt a big chunk of my heart drive away with him. When my boy walked out the door, I knew he would be gone for a long time. I had a powerful sense of free-falling into unknown territory. I'd been on a nonstop roller coaster ride with a scream stuck in my throat for the past few years.

While Chris was in the Utah desert, I prayed the desert sun would bake away his disease. I consciously tried to leave behind all the desperate nights I'd spent trying to track him down, the fear I'd been carrying, and the times he'd pushed me away.

Joe and I had weekly phone calls with Chris and his therapist, Ben. The first week Chris was away, Ben shared with us the results of Chris's screening and assessment. What a wake-up call for me. Having prided myself on being a parent with her eyes wide open, I was thrown. Chris had been smoking weed daily, using pills whenever possible, and he'd been selling them. He'd reported feeling unhappy for a long time. It was hard to absorb the information we received. I felt foolish for being in denial and not realizing how bad things had gotten, and I also felt vindicated that I hadn't been overreacting.

Ben gave us assignments. The first was to write an impact letter to Chris. We were to send Ben our letters so he could review them before reading them to Chris in the presence of his peers. I didn't want to give Chris the "tough love" the program advised, encouraging brutal honesty, but I agreed to do whatever might get his attention.

At the end of the call, Ben asked if he could talk to me alone. The connection was lousy from up in the mountains, in and out, but I heard Ben clearly say, "Listen, Sally. This will be hard to hear, but I know you can handle it. I need you to know that Chris told me he is not as comfortable with you as he is with his dad."

"I was afraid he felt that way," I told him, unsurprised by this information even though it slayed me. "I know that he isn't interested in anything I have to say. I've been feeling so defeated."

"No, what you say matters, Sally." I want to cry, and I'm glad Joe has left the room. "He thinks you have given up because you just don't get involved anymore."

"Oh my God. I AM involved. Just behind the scenes. I don't want to get mad at him or let him see my frustration, so I always encourage Joe to talk to him. I think he hears it better if it's coming from him." I know I'm being defensive, but I can't stop myself from asserting, "I am involved. Very involved."

It feels like a sword is lodged in my throat, and I quiet down. Deeply hurt and off balance, I'm defeated thinking about all the time and energy I wasted strategizing to get Joe up to speed. Ben tries to reassure me that I will be better able to reach Chris if I can be more honest with him. Through the static on the line, I hear him say, "Remember, Sally, kids don't respond well when we operate from fear. I bet Chris can sense yours, which may be why he hasn't wanted you to get too close even if you tried." Talk about the truth. I know he's right. I'm both grateful for his directness and filled with shame.

I hang up quickly and begin the assignment right away. Head in my hands, I try to move beyond my own hurt and find a way to help Chris see the effects of his addiction on me, our relationship, and our family. My script slants on the page as my frustration bubbles to the surface. I start to realize the lengths I've gone to to avoid being angry. It hadn't occurred to me that sparing Chris from my anger was dishonest. I see now how I've wanted to avoid being like my explosive, frightening father.

It feels mean, but now that I've been encouraged to express my anger, I can't stop:

You never have anything nice to say to your brother and sister. I'm afraid you might hurt your little brother out of anger. There is no excuse for your behavior. You don't make any contribution to our family or give a shit about anyone other than yourself. You have the audacity to complain about what we do for you, and you put up a wall.

I put my pen down and back away from my desk, wondering if what I've just written will hurt him the same way he has hurt me. There's so much I haven't dared say—until now. I'm extra mad after hearing that he thinks I've given up.

He has no idea how I really feel. I will never give up. Ever. I sit back down and keep writing:

Whenever I tried to get you to go to school or do your homework, we'd end up arguing. I would find myself yelling at you and hate myself for it. That's when I resigned to have Dad enforce things with you because otherwise, it became a power struggle.

I read over what I've written and continue:

I am afraid you are going to die. I don't want to lose you. And I don't ever feel like I really have you. I am always missing you if that makes any sense. I wish you knew how much I adore you.

I worry, knowing you are drinking, doing drugs, and making reckless decisions. I can't sleep until I know you are home safely. And despite all this I know that I am basically just an annoyance to you. I get in the way of your partying, and you just want me off your back. The worst part is when you lie to my face.

I see how personally I've taken Chris's behavior. How rejected I've felt. How disrespected. I've not realized how much his disease is the one doing the talking. But I also see how much I've been missing him even when he's home. I've tried and failed to have the kind of closeness with him I want to have.

After Chris got my impact letter, he wrote back. He told me our relationship hadn't gotten better when I gave him more space. Instead, he felt that our relationship had just "gone away." It was devastating to have him think I'd given up. I took what Chris said to heart. I blamed myself entirely for all the difficulty in our relationship and didn't appreciate, until later, the role of his addiction in causing me to feel such helplessness. I see now how I was putting my energy into something I couldn't control as opposed to what I could. The only thing I could control was me.

In the weeks that followed, I began to try to recalibrate. Knowing Chris was clean and sober provided some of the relief I hadn't known I needed so badly. It gave me the chance to think about all of what led up to his being there. I wished I could start over and parent him more effectively. And at the same time, I knew deep down there was not a single thing that could have offset his powerful predisposition toward addiction.

seventeen

*I*t's first thing in the morning and, upon awakening, I go right into a quiet time. I have a longstanding routine of beginning my day with several prayers, adding my daily lesson from *A Course in Miracles* to my ritual, as I need all the help I can get. There's a small gallery of photos of my children on my bedside table that I can easily turn to with my head resting on my pillow. In its center is a photo of Christopher and me at a pool in Arizona. Our heads are touching, and it's here where I'm reminded how much he resembled me more than my other kids. Our skin, the exact same shade of red and tan, shines in the sunlight. Our button noses peek out from beneath our sunglasses.

I extend my left arm out toward his photo as if reaching toward him in the flesh. I'm convinced Chris brought me the solace my daily lessons offer, but before I read them, I send each of my children love and light beginning with him. Sometimes, after reaching toward his picture, I close my eyes and let the image of Chris's face linger, causing me to smile. Sometimes I just holler in my head, *I love you so fucking much,* as an arrow of pain plunges into my chest. I turn my head to send prayers to my girl in the middle, then turn again to my right to send them to my youngest. Generally, I try not to worry about Caroline

and William, actively trying to embrace *The Serenity Prayer*. I
have come to believe nothing good comes from fear, which my
morning lessons affirm. Having always been a "do-er," praying
for my children helps me feel like there is something I can do
as their mother—a way to feel less powerless. A spoonful of
sugar and a wave of my wand are proof I'm giving them something, even if it never feels like it's enough.

Once out of bed, I open my bottom dresser drawer to put
my nightgown away. My friends have said things like, "You got
out of bed. You're ahead of the game." They're right. Tucked in
the back corners of the drawer are my children's baby blankets.
No one knows that they're there or that from time to time I like
to reach back toward Christopher's white one, dotted with tiny
blue flowers, and hold it between my fingers and thumb and rub
it the way I rub Cassidy's ear, relishing its softness. My plan was
to save the blanket, gift-wrap it, and give it back to him before he
got married.

I'm generally working on giving myself permission to do
whatever I need to do to survive. If that means sneaking a hold
of my son's baby blanket for comfort whenever I want to, so be
it. Taking care of myself better than I ever have is a priority now.

It is a white-skied summer day at the beginning of August. Since
I wasn't called into work today, I sit right outside our sliding
door in the Adirondack chair planted under the wind chimes.
The sun blazes hot, and the chimes are still. I recall the summer
Chris was in the wilderness and how I forced myself into a self-
care regimen. Adding self-help meetings for family members to
my own recovery meetings taught me to shift my focus from trying to control my son's addiction to checking in with myself
emotionally. It's when I started to recognize how pervasive and

powerful my fear had become and slowly began to ask myself what I needed to feel more grounded and balanced. Less frantic.

While Chris was at the wilderness program, I started to get honest about the impact of his addiction on me. As the daughter of an alcoholic, I'd become wired to walk on eggshells. I couldn't trust Chris or myself. No wonder I'd been keeping my distance. My fear had been running interference. Our bond was damaged, and I wanted desperately to restore it. Only when I was able to get real with myself about how difficult it was for me to parent Chris did I begin to see things clearly. His addiction and my loyalty to him had prevented me from admitting that I didn't always like how he behaved. But I always loved him. Having some space to recognize how burdened I'd felt and how scared I was enabled me to ease up on myself and step beyond my shame so I could think about who I wanted to be as Chris's mother from that point forward. I began focusing on simply letting Chris know how much he was loved.

I dug deeper in therapy. "No one gets it," I complained to my therapist at the time, Mary Ann. "This damn addiction happened to Chris so fast I couldn't keep up, and at the same time it happened slowly, like I was watching a train fly into a wall and couldn't do anything to stop it."

"Why do you always think it's all up to you?" Mary Ann challenged.

"It just is . . ." I started and stopped. I didn't feel like going into my past even though I knew it was necessary, so I sunk lower into my chair and looked out at Millennium Park from her office building window. "Ever since I was young, I've felt old . . ."

Before I could say anything more, she asked, "What was it about your childhood experience that led you to feel so hyper-responsible and alone?"

I looked up at her rosy cheeks and serious expression. I sat back up, knowing she wanted me to take this seriously too. I told her about how I'd grown up fast like many children of alcoholics do. As the oldest, I'd concluded it was my job to take care of things, especially after my parents' divorce. It was my job to make everybody feel better. The more I shared, the more I could see how I'd brought this outsized sense of duty to my role as a parent, as well as the self-imposed pressure to break out from a family legacy of addiction.

"I think I decided a long time ago that it was my job to prevent Chris from becoming an alcoholic. To save his life." As I say it out loud, I realize how I have always assumed the responsibility of protecting him from himself. "Wow. If I continue to seriously feel like everything is up to me, I'm not letting him live his life and learn his own life lessons. It's hard to let go of control when the stakes are so high."

Mary Ann nodded. "It sure is."

I rise from the Adirondack chair and wipe the sweat from my brow. I need to get into the air-conditioning. It is both excruciating and healing to relive what it was like that summer we sent Chris away at sixteen. It's also hard to believe it's been six long years since he went to Wilderness. I recognize that the investment in self-care back then laid the foundation for what I need to do now. My emotional well-being has got to come first. I must tap back into my faith to offset the surge of fear that re-emerged when Chris died. I want to find a way to make things make sense, and I hope that writing into the past and into the pain will help me find a way not to be so hard on myself by assuming all the responsibility.

While away at Wilderness, Chris revealed in his letters so much that he hadn't been able to express to us before. He shared how he wanted to escape his feelings of low self-esteem and self-consciousness with alcohol and drugs. He wrote that he was depressed, unmotivated, and angry. He also wrote that he was proud of what he was doing and that he wanted to change. I knew changing would be a long process and that his feelings would be all over the place as he went through withdrawal.

During this time, Joe and I communicated a lot with our educational consultant, Kim, and Chris's therapist, Ben, about what would happen once he completed the wilderness program. He wanted to come home, but Kim emphasized that he should not return to the same environment where he developed his addiction. Joe and I agreed. This was just the beginning of his recovery journey. The next step would be to locate a therapeutic boarding school that would give him the support he needed to maintain his sobriety and address any lingering depression.

As the weeks passed, we struggled to make a choice. The stakes *were* life and death, and there *was* a sense of urgency. We had just two years to seize the opportunity to save his life. Kim made it very clear to us that once he turned eighteen, we would lose any legal power we held, which activated more fear. I kept trying to let go so that I could finally let him get down to his own work of getting better.

We decided on a therapeutic boarding school in Arizona called In Balance Ranch Academy. Chris could complete high school there and receive ongoing recovery support on a ranch, which, for Joe and me as riders and horse lovers, held a certain appeal as it implied work and play.

When we informed him of our decision, he said, "Let me get this straight: You're going to send me from the desert to the desert?"

It took discipline for us to hold the line and insist that he try it out. We were doing what we felt we had to do. We certainly didn't tell him that it would cost everything we had set aside for his college or that we were intentionally placing him in an all-boys environment to avoid what would certainly be too big a distraction for my boy. His primary interest at sixteen was whether girls would be there.

Eight weeks after Chris left for Utah, Joe and I flew to Salt Lake City to pick him up. My goal was to be present and loving. When we arrived, we gathered in a hotel conference room along with four other sets of parents and some of the program staff. We awkwardly sat down around a table, all of us appearing bedraggled as if we, like our children, had been in the wilderness for several months.

When we were encouraged to introduce ourselves, most of us hesitated, but not Joe. He launched right in. "I've been in recovery a long time, and I looked at my son one day and saw myself at the end of my drinking when I thought taking my life might be my only way out." The other parents stared at him, but before they could respond, Joe blurted, "So we had to do something, and that's why he's here!" I appreciated how Joe always seemed willing to break the ice, typically with small talk, setting people at ease. At the same time, even though I value going deep since it's all I can do, it was hard for me to see him get vulnerable, his guilt and fear so exposed. Everyone else appeared to let out a breath and seemed grateful he'd been so open. I was surprised that my tough guy of a husband had been willing to share that he had been suicidal. It sunk in that he had not just been thinking about the brothers he'd lost but of his own experience, which I had somehow conveniently forgotten. He identified more than ever with Christopher and had been recalling his own pain while our son went through this experience. The wounds of his past exacerbated his own fear.

The next day we drove out to Chris's campsite in the Uinta mountains to spend his last night in the wilderness program with him. The staff forewarned us that he was still angry and that he might not have much to say.

Midmorning we jumped out of the truck, expecting to see Chris right away. Instead, we stood in the dirt with the sun beating down on us, looking out at the desert mountains awash in peach and copper hues. We were given bandannas and instructed to put them over our eyes. One end of a long rope was placed in our hands. They told us that Chris was at the other end, guiding us to an unknown destination. I tripped over rocks and stumbled along. I couldn't bear not being able to see my boy after all this time. But the intention was clear: We were meant to understand how he must have felt when he arrived eight weeks ago. And we were being asked to trust him for the first time in a long time.

Finally, we were told we could untie our bandannas. I yanked mine from my face and waited for my eyes to adjust.

There he was. With dirt under his fingernails and shaggy, greasy hair in his eyes, Christopher was gorgeous to me. He didn't have much to say, as expected, but I could tell that neither a drink nor a drug had crossed his lips in two months. The sparkle was back in his eyes. Along with it, a touch of tenderness, maybe even contentment, shone on his tanned face. I realized in that moment that his heart and soul had been hiding, and now his light was turned back on. He had a gentle glow, and I turned to it. Along with his glow was a flicker of warmth. I drew closer.

It felt so good just to be near him. We sat in the dust, and he showed us how to "bust a flame." He used a stick he had carved into a bow with a piece of string attached to it to create enough friction to start a fire. Before long, it generated sparks that he breathed life into. A proud smile, which I hadn't seen in a long time, lit up his face as he explained that it hadn't been easy to learn.

"Want to try it, Mom?" He handed the softened stick to me. I tried to get a fire going, but it was going to require far more patience and perseverance than I could muster. "Honey, no way I can do this. It's crazy hard. You made it look like a breeze!" I smiled as I handed it back, relieved to let him lead the way. Just being together was such a gift. Loving him felt easy again.

That evening, Chris cooked us a meal over the fire. Salty rice with blackened vegetables never tasted so good as Joe and I witnessed Chris's satisfaction in showing us what he could do.

We took a hike, and Chris warned me about scorpions, confidently lifting rocks where they might be hiding. We explored the red clay rocks and dry terrain, and he pointed out ancient markings on the rocky mountain wall.

As the sky began to darken, I joked, "So where's the bathroom?" There was no bathroom, no tent, not even any pillows. Just rolled up sleeping bags, one for each of us. As evening fell, we unrolled them. Joe and I laid ours on either side of Christopher.

I felt the rocks pushing into my back as I lay there listening to my son breathe. It had been a good day. The air was pure and crisp, the sky a velvety midnight blue. Other families were spread out somewhere on the mountain, but it felt as if we were the only people on earth. There were so many stars brightly piercing the vast, dreamy mural above us. Suspended in time, I was offered a one-night reprieve before I'd have to let my son go again.

I refused to think about the next day in Arizona when we'd have to say goodbye. I swept aside my dread and made a quiet vow to keep doing whatever it took to stop his addiction from taking him away from me and prayed what we were doing now would bring him closer.

"Good night, my precious boy. Sweet dreams. Momma loves you," I whispered as I drifted off into a deep sleep I didn't think would come so quickly.

eighteen

*I*t's a Friday on a late afternoon in August, over seven months since Chris died. After huddling in the hall with my coworkers at the end of a long day, I'm leaving work. I take the elevator down to the lower level of the hospital and cut through the cafeteria to the shuttle. It's empty except for a few folks behind the register and a janitor collecting trays off the tables. I stop to see if they have any of those melt-in-your-mouth freshly baked chocolate chip cookies for the taking, and they do. My sugar addiction is alive and well. You can basically track my weight and its direct correlation to stress over the years. Twenty pounds on when my cortisol was firing, twenty pounds off again when I knew my child was safe and sound. Back up now as my grief insists on comfort and food as the only form of self-medication I have left.

I'm aware that my whole body has been penetrated by grief. The brain fog that must be shock-related precludes me from recalling people's names. I have prided myself on never forgetting names, but now my short-term memory has short-circuited. My doctor advised me to get a stress test on my heart a few weeks ago. I laughed. She wanted to rule things out since I've had a wheeze that won't let up, but I'm pretty sure my heart is fine. Just shattered.

Nervous when they placed the electrodes on my chest, I brought Chris with me. He gives me strength. My heart is healthy, apparently, but I only just discovered there is such a thing as broken heart syndrome, and grieving people have died from it. I'm not surprised. I will never again underestimate the impact of emotion on one's health. My grief, at best, is a layer of melancholy with long, smoky fingers, a dementor of insidious darkness. A constant undercurrent in my days. I feel the lines forming on my face, and it isn't from being middle-aged. It's as if my tears have dug ruts into my skin. If I look at a picture of myself before Chris died versus now, I see that my eyes have become haunted. And I'm not just being dramatic.

The morning after we slept out beneath the stars, Joe, Chris, and I broke camp and headed to the wilderness program's Salt Lake City offices for showers. We got Chris a haircut, did some shopping, and then drove to Tucson, where we spent the night. Chris wolfed down a big dinner, jumped in the pool, and stayed up all night watching movies with Joe. I wanted to join them, but I was already aching over the impending drop-off the next day.

I tried to keep my dread at bay as we drove down to In Balance Ranch in Huachuca, but I felt uneasy. My chest fluttered as we flew down the highway. As we neared our destination, the area felt desolate. We had landed in the middle of nowhere. I prayed the risk we were taking would be worth it.

I wondered if we were lost when we turned off onto the long, winding desert road. This was not where I'd ever envisioned taking my son. It was as if we'd stumbled onto the set of an old Western movie. Not far from Tombstone itself, we pulled up to what would be Chris's new home. I began to add a wash of color to the image I'd already built of the ranch in my mind. The deep sky was where most of the color lay, and everything else my eyes landed on was scrubbed in browns, peaches, and sandy tones. We were greeted by several young men who welcomed Chris and gave us a tour. Despite the warm, easy feel of the place, I felt as parched as the dusty ground beneath my feet.

It occurred to me that Chris would be bored here. No phones, no video games, no girls. I looked at the wooden deck outside Chris's room, where boys' cowboy boots were strewn, and crossed my fingers that he would find a way to settle in.

We toured the rustic dining hall and went into the class-rooms, housed in a separate building. All too soon we ran out of things to see. We'd seen the basketball courts and the outdoor ping-pong table and briefly sat on the big brown leather couches on either side of the pool table in the lounge. It was time to let go again.

Chris had always been so comfortable racing out the door, but this time I felt him hesitate to leave our side. The three of us stood beneath a bare little tree facing a fenced-in pasture. We didn't have words for this goodbye. I looked out at the horses, their necks sunk low in their troughs, and the sky so big it swallowed us up, and was overcome by a painful surrender. I put on my brave face, not allowing myself to feel the familiar pang of missing him as I hugged him hard, my arms wrapped around his shoulders, head against his chest. After I let go, I walked straight to the car without looking back as he'd so often done.

Sitting at my laptop in our breakfast room on a Sunday, I am about to begin writing when I hear a bird outside our screen chirp and chirp ceaselessly. I look to see if it's one of the little family of sparrows living between our downspout and the roof. From their nest packed full of grass and twigs, I often hear the demands of the babies tucked inside—"cheep, cheep, cheeps" interspersed between the windchime's breezy verse. I step out onto our deck to look up at the little nest. It appears empty, but I continue to hear a chirping from above. I walk out further to discover a dead baby bird that's fallen to the ground, and its mama, sitting perched in the walnut tree overhead, continues to call for it, yearning for it to wake up.

This mama bird and my fellow bereaved mothers carry an emptiness that is so gaping it takes over. The pain is so great I ask myself how it's possible that so many of us could be living with it. It is simply unfathomable. The mama bird sounds her alarm, and I am sobbing with all of the mothers who've withstood the suffering and death of their babies from physical illness, the mothers who've felt the despair of losing their sons and daughters to the devastation of suicide, the increasing masses of mothers whose children have been taken by the opioid epidemic, by murder, or accident—and any and all of the other ways mothers could lose their children that I have failed to include. I ache for us all.

I am often asked if I communicate with the mothers of the boys who died alongside Christopher that day. I sent them my condolences immediately, but I only really knew one other mom and her son and didn't know them well, even though he and Chris were good friends. I pray for each of these moms and their beloved sons, but we do not talk. It feels impossible to absorb our pain multiplied. We each move through our personal grief on our own private islands of despair, unable to face any more trauma as we try to survive our own. I return to sitting at our big farm table inside and try to resume writing about Chris's time at the ranch.

Lyndsey was a "safe friend" who was permitted to be in communication with him while he was at In Balance. She had asked him to the Turnabout dance in the Spring of their freshman year. She told me he would call her regularly to talk about his horse, Emma. She said, "Chris's sense of humor often had those close to him trying to decipher fact from fiction, so naturally, at first, I had my doubts that Emma was real. I still laugh thinking about how much he loved that horse. He loved what he loved—Justin Bieber, Hawaiian shirts, his friends and family, and even a horse named Emma, unashamedly and wholeheartedly. He recycled love. However much he was and is loved—an immense amount—he made sure to put even more love and kindness back into the world."

I experience this recycling every time I get to spend time with his friends. I'm able to love them with all the leftover love I have for Chris. When we are included in what is happening in their lives, it is a gift. When I get to hug them, hear their stories, and look them in the eyes, it is the closest I get to having him here in a body. They are an extension of Chris and bring him to life. Getting to love them sustains me.

After dropping Chris off, we couldn't see him again until the beginning of September, when the first family weekend was scheduled. We took Caroline and William out of school for a couple of days so we could all be together. Despite heading to the airport early, an accident caused us to be late for our flight, so Joe had to stay behind to bring our luggage the next day.

Without anything but the clothes on our backs, we landed in Tucson, checked into the hotel, and then raced to the ranch. Six weeks had passed without seeing him. We'd had weekly calls with him and his therapist, but it wasn't enough. I had to see him right away, even knowing it would be a race against time to get there before curfew. Feeling awful about pulling Caroline and

William out of school, I now felt even worse dragging them along with me on the drive to Huachuca. I underestimated how long the drive would take and overestimated my ability to see at night. Arizona's monsoon season floods made for cracked and rutted clay that our rental car bounced over too quickly. It was pitch black, and I didn't have any depth perception. Desperate to get there in time and fearing we were too late, I stopped when we finally got to the iron cattle gate, reflecting the white-silver light of the moon. I lowered my window and hurriedly announced that we had come to see Chris. A glimpse was all we got. Stepping out from the shadows, browned by the desert sun, all there was time for was a look into his eyes and a quick big hug. And I would make that drive again. A million times over. Even after discovering the bumper of the rental car dangling over its front wheels when we got back to our hotel.

The next morning, our first day of family weekend, we hurried to join the other families in a big meeting room. We had been given an assignment to complete ahead of time, and it was the first thing on the agenda. We were partnered up with another family and sent to a separate room. They looked like a mirror image of our family, with their oldest son at the ranch and a younger sister and brother visiting too. Joe wasn't going to make it in time for this exercise, but we were proceeding ahead.

Each of us in the room was directed, one at a time, to sit in front of our family member and present our "list work," a fill-in-the-blanks assignment designed to help us clearly identify how his addictive behavior had affected us.

My heart squeezed as I watched the mother of the family we'd been partnered with sitting across from her son. I winced in sympathy as she struggled to get the words out. She was vulnerable but didn't cry.

When it was my turn, I felt certain I'd break down in tears.

Chris had his head down as I pulled my chair across from his until our knees almost touched.

While this exercise had the same objective as the impact letter I'd written when he was at the wilderness program, the goal here was for it to be like family therapy where we could speak the truth and do some healing. But it was hard to write and extremely hard to say out loud to Christopher in front of this other family and my other kids.

I read from the worksheet on my lap in a whisper. "WHEN YOU . . . lie to me repeatedly, LIKE . . . any time I ask you where you are, I FEEL . . . deceived, hurt, and foolish." I looked up at my son's stoic face briefly and continued, my voice rising. "WHEN you . . . avoid spending time with us, LIKE . . . when you will do anything not to be home or shut yourself in your room, I FEEL . . . unimportant, sad, and lonely."

Chris didn't respond. He just sat and listened. I finished reading my responses and stepped away, feeling numb, fighting back all emotion, and trying to be strong.

We went back and forth between families, each member addressing the addict until everyone had borne witness to their pain.

Fourteen-year-old Caroline tried to articulate her hurt, which ran deep. "It's hard when you're around," she began. "You mostly just ignore me because I'm a girl." She had her chair pushed back, and I could see how hard she was trying to say what she needed to without betraying her big brother or making him angry. I watched her scoot her chair back and wrap her arms around her waist for protection. She was often kinder to Chris than he'd been able to be to her. I knew that in Chris's eyes, everything came more easily to her, especially school, and he resented it. He couldn't see Caroline clearly enough to appreciate that she had struggles of her own.

William, just ten years old, was the last to go. He sank down in his chair and read the words he had scrawled out in big letters. "Chris, when you took money from my piggy bank and I asked you if you stole it and you said you didn't, I didn't have any money left and you lied . . ." Sobs erupted from everyone in the room before William could finish. It killed me to watch my sweet William admit his disappointment in his much older brother, whom he continued to worship. Chris didn't cry, but he couldn't look any of us in the eye.

As soon as William finished, we were rushed off to lunch. Joe arrived just in time to join us for sandwiches. I felt beyond wrung out already. Caroline and William had shown up bravely and been so vulnerable. It filled me with pain and pride, and at the same time I questioned whether the staff knew what they were doing by subjecting them to such heartache. I was hurting so much on my younger children's behalf that I didn't think about how Chris must have felt listening to our tough love. Instead, I was focused on what his siblings had gone through. The exercise provoked more feeling than I could tolerate, especially since my children's pain was my own. As we left the room, I tried to maintain trust in the professionals as they guided our family in our healing process.

Over the next several days, our family participated in numerous team-building exercises. In an equine therapy session, they brought a horse into the ring where we stood. A low wooden jump was placed on the other side. To develop our problem-solving skills, we were tasked with getting the horse to step over the jump without touching her. Joe stepped in immediately and tried to get the horse to move with the force of his will. The big bay mare just stood there stubbornly as the other families watched us from outside the ring.

I felt self-conscious and I knew Chris did too. He stood off to the side in the dust, shaking his head as Joe became frustrated. I watched him shut down while I attempted to encourage the other kids to participate by shooing them with my arms. I wiped the sweat from my forehead and stood on the other side of the jump, beckoning the big-bellied mare to come join me. The more frustrated Joe got, the more pressure I felt to make something happen. The hot sun magnified my helplessness. Time slowed. I stared at her, hoping she could read my mind, but knew she wasn't going to budge and desperately wanted her to do something, anything. If I could just cajole her to take a step in that direction, I knew I'd feel less desperate. We continued playing our parts: Joe trying to force things, Chris quiet with an inner storm brewing, Caroline trying to take care of her little brother who kept talking, and me, embarrassed by our ineffectiveness, just hoping to show the families watching that there was nothing wrong with us and needing to show them what I hadn't been able to prove at home—that I had some semblance of control.

That weekend I discovered how similar all the boys at the ranch were. We mothers compared notes and shook our heads as we shared about how each of them bucked the boundaries and rules of a sober life. They all complained about the food. They wanted to pierce their ears, get tattoos, and sneak cigarettes. Give them an inch and they'd take a mile. Many of them were extroverted and risk-takers like Chris, who drank and took drugs in the camaraderie of a pack. Others were socially anxious and creative boys who abused alcohol and drugs in isolation. All of them struggled to self-regulate. Like me, the other mothers were frazzled and fearful and saw no other way to help their boys than sending them to the ranch. It was reassuring not to feel alone or ashamed as I often did at home, certain I was the only mother incapable of controlling her child. We connected over our desperation and our hope.

nineteen

I've taken the top off my jeep and again find myself on a late August afternoon driving to the grave, looking for my son as if he's still here. The bright sun shining, the wind in my hair, the music loud, he's along for the ride. I experience a moment of freedom from despair, the joy he brings. "Hi, babe," I whisper as I look at his picture on my dashboard and listen to Jason Aldean's "A Little More Summertime." Like many songs, its chords pluck at my insides. I want more of him. Christopher *was* my summertime. Yes, he was a handful, but Chris brought me home to myself. Without him here, I can't know peace.

I turn off the road toward the cemetery, asking myself how August has already come. Sensing the inevitable fade of my favorite season, I am extra soulful, as if losing summer means losing Christopher all over again. He is closest when I am enjoying summer's simple pleasures. A bite of cool watermelon, juice dribbling down my chin, checkered tablecloths, short skirts, sea glass, and buckets of sand. Such light-hearted associations compete with my pain. As the season closes, breaking up the seemingly endless blank skies of midwestern winter, I realize it feels just as it did to have Chris here—too good to last.

My missing of him is a song in a round. I'm stuck in a spiral of relentless mourning. Not until his death did I mourn his babyhood, his childhood, his adolescence, and his college years. One might think we would be acclimated to grief as mothers. There is a cumulative series of goodbyes at each milestone. Our generation not only celebrates each development, but we literally congratulate our kids for growing up. Our children shape-shift, and the years fly by with a whisper of grief along the way if we stop to notice it. But we rarely do. My heart is tugged at every age and stage without respite. Nothing lasts, nothing stays the same.

I experience a jolt of longing. Loooonnnnging. It begins in the crux of grief's shadow, firing into my nerve endings where it radiates. I remember all that I was lucky enough to have during his twenty-one years, and superimposed on these layers of loss is also the loss of the future. What does the future hold now? Is this how it's meant to be? I'm still falling, and I don't know if I will ever land. I pull into the circular drive, get out of my jeep, and beeline for Christopher's gravestone beyond the large cross midway to the trees in the back.

I sit down in the grass and clover beneath his gravestone and think about how so much that is beautiful is also fleeting. My son, the summer, the lilies of the valley that popped up along our fence this spring, pungent and fresh one day, the next day gone.

After performing my ritual of securing his mementos around his stone, wiping it clean of dirt and grass, and rubbing my hand across his name, I am back in my jeep in just fifteen minutes. These visits are quick, just as our phone calls once were —a moment to connect before I get too filled with a missing that overtakes me. I turn up the volume. Music has been an invitation throughout my life, evoking feelings and bringing them to the surface. Now every song I hear becomes a love song, and each one takes me to Christopher. There is a new meaning in the lyrics of heartbreak. My pain is raw and enveloping, breaking through my numbness and connecting me to Chris's intensely alive spirit, adding a tingle of excitement and that hint of elation only he can offer. I listen to a playlist of his favorite songs, and they help me feel moved by his enthusiasm for life. I go back in time to my own youthful exuberance and recognize the "me" in Chris, the "me" I was before I became a mom and let my fear overtake me. The songs are carefree, light, and breezy. Soothing or upbeat, there is a vast array of music he loved. Will collected Chris's favorites from his friends, and I added my own. My personalized ringtone for Chris was the guitar strum. If I hear it now on someone else's phone, it throws me. But it perfectly captures my son's effect on my heart.

My Christopher song was Sheryl Crow's version of "Sweet Child O' Mine" because of her gorgeous voice, because of the strings, and the beauty of the notes, but mostly for the plea of the deeper question the song asks. I think about where my son has gone and where I'm going and conclude there is nothing like music to match the bittersweet power of my grief.

After the family weekend at In Balance Ranch Academy, I decided not to go more than six weeks between visits with Chris. I couldn't be away from him for longer, and I was focused on rebuilding our relationship. Joe and I took turns traveling to Arizona while the other held down the fort at home. The whole family went to the ranch for Thanksgiving, and since Chris wasn't allowed home for Christmas, I went to him. It was a gift to have one-on-one time together. We settled into an easy rhythm where I no longer had a sense of urgency and could relinquish control, allowing more joy into our relationship. What a privilege it became to steal quality time with him like this, without distraction.

Waking up to Christopher asleep in the bed next to me in our hotel room was the only Christmas present I needed that year. He opened his eyes and looked down at the stack of wrapped presents waiting for him on the floor between us. "Merry Christmas, my angel! Ready to open some presents?" I called from under my covers.

I didn't need to rouse him from sleep. He popped up against his pillows and called out, "Merry Christmas, Momma!" He winked at me as he reached down to grab his gifts and place them in his lap. As he began to rip the paper, I was reminded of his wide-eyed look of wonder as a little boy on Christmas morning when he spotted Santa's footprints in the soot of our fireplace. His thrill when he saw the presents Santa brought under the tree. Now at sixteen, he ripped into the box with the same exuberance. Once he saw what it was, he put his arms through the sleeves of his new Buffalo Bills Jersey. Then he gave me one of his crooked, knowing smiles, jumped off the bed, and gave me a hug,

"Mom, you're the bomb. This is awesome. GO BILLS!" he yelled as he peered down at the white buffalo on his chest.

"Dad and I picked out the color. I'm so glad you like it. It's soooo cute on you."

He nodded, and I relished his satisfaction. His joy was mine.

It was strange to be in the desert on Christmas with no snow, and there weren't a lot of restaurants open in Tucson. So, we spent the day at the hotel, where I watched Chris play pool. I beamed as he showed me how good he'd become. By then I'd begun to fill him in bit by bit about my own experience getting sober. He didn't seem surprised after all, and it felt to me like it brought us closer. I wanted to be real and unashamed. We even attended some meetings together, which was amazing for me and less than amazing for him. That was clear when, at our first meeting together, I sat down, and he walked across the room. I felt a tiny pang in my chest, but I understood how uncool it would be, at sixteen, to sit next to your mom. No matter how cool I thought I still was.

It was such a relief to discover Chris was in good hands at the ranch. He let me know over and over he wasn't thrilled to be there, but I could tell he wasn't miserable either. He'd come to love horses, particularly his horse, Emma, a painted pinto whom he'd been assigned to care for. When Chris won the ranch Gymkhana competition with Emma, his excitement bounced through the phone line on one of our weekly calls. There was a dreamy, bright blue-sky comfort I experienced over those twelve months he spent as a student at In Balance. Joe and I felt connected to his therapist, the owners, and many of the boys and their families at the ranch.

While this period felt relatively peaceful, the fear popped up that Chris might not stay sober post-treatment. We did not yet know what he'd do next. It was a lot easier not to worry while he was away, but my nervous system was still hijacked, and it could be set off by preparing for his permitted short visits when he would be hanging out with old friends or, by his insistence on pushing boundaries, even when sober.

One family weekend we'd showed up for, we arrived only to find out he wasn't allowed off the ranch, having been caught smoking cigars with another ranch boy. It was always something. Even while he was there, I remained in a state of suspension, waiting for the next incident to thwart any glimpse of peace I might have thought I had. Chris's addiction had an invisible but powerful impact on me, with my worry depleting my ability to be my best for Caroline and William.

Fourteen, and stuck between two brothers who demanded my emotional and physical attention, Caroline had a refreshing degree of self-sufficiency. I was so grateful she didn't struggle academically and did what she was told. I know I wasn't as available to her as she deserved. When my only un-squeaky wheel became angry and acted as if she didn't want me around, I began to walk on eggshells with her just as I had with Chris. Patterns I picked up as a little girl in response to my dad's shifting moods were hard to break.

William, at eleven, put the H in ADHD and kept me on my toes as his older brother had. But differently. He never slept well, which caused him to miss some school, but his teachers didn't seem concerned about his academic performance—at least not yet. He channeled his energy into athletics, and I relished being able to drive him to his hockey, football, and lacrosse games. His travel schedules were demanding, but I savored the fact that he still wanted me around, knowing how fleeting it would be.

Christopher's addiction deeply affected me emotionally, as revealed when Joe and I visited Chris together in the late spring of 2011 after he'd been away from home for a year. It was a hot day in Tucson, and the three of us decided to head to a cool movie theater for an afternoon showing of *The Fighter*.

We got our popcorn and drinks and plopped into the theater seats, with Chris between me and Joe. It wouldn't have mattered what was playing. I just savored how comfortable it felt now to be in Chris's presence. He was developing more confidence with every month of sobriety he put under his belt. I felt it radiating from him when we were close.

About halfway through the movie, I gripped the armrests of my seat. On the screen, a mother pounded on the door of a run-down house. I identified with her unease as she called out for her son who was an addict. He saw her coming and jumped out of an upstairs window to escape getting caught using. I turned to look at Chris, who was staring intently as the main character landed in a dumpster out back. The mother's face crumpled as she realized her son had been getting high. I knew her anguish as she turned away from the crack house and walked back to her car.

A sob escaped from my throat in a whimper when the son opened the passenger door and sat down next to her. I willed myself not to look at Chris as the son began to sing a sweet plea to his mother for her forgiveness.

The portrayal of her adoration and despair pulled me into the depths of my own, including the feelings I hadn't even permitted myself to have up until that moment. I recognized immediately the eggshell walk between fear and defeat, killed softly as I watched the son charm his mother the same way Christopher always charmed me.

Chris placed his arm around my shoulders and gave me a squeeze. When I finally turned to look at him, he met my eyes. I could see he felt compassion for what he'd put me through. For the first time, I felt deeply seen by him. It affirmed that the sacrifice of sending him away had been worth it. He was back to being my sweet, loving boy.

On a cool September afternoon, eight months after Chris died, his girlfriend Gali and I meet at a nearby Starbucks. To me, she is still his girlfriend even though they broke up after he turned nineteen and left Arizona. They started dating each other when he was thirteen and she was twelve, and they continued to see each other for about a year. Her family moved to Arizona in 2011, and as soon as he was granted permission to communicate from In Balance Ranch, they reconnected. They were then together again until he relapsed in June of 2013.

A week before our meeting, I'd found myself wanting to talk to her. I knew it would be hard for us both, so I also found myself hesitating to arrange it. Chris must have been prompting me to set it up, so I reached out. Gali had attended his wake and funeral, but I wasn't sure I'd seen her. That time period is extra blurry for me, consisting of fractious images of who I saw and what was said, my shock fading my memory.

When I walk in the door, she's already sitting down. I'd forgotten how pretty she is. Long blonde hair, dancer legs, and bright blue eyes. My son's first and longest love. Oh, their breakup had been brutal to witness. It was complicated and messy. I hated that it ended the way it did.

Gali timidly stands up and I give her the biggest hug. I feel shy too. "It's so good to see you, Gal," I begin.

"You, too, Mrs. McQuillen. Chris has been on my mind so much. I have been wanting to let you know how guilty I've been feeling. I hate that our relationship ended the way it did." It is hard to believe their breakup happened three years ago, in the spring of 2013, and here we are in the fall of 2016. Her hair is covering her face as she looks down at her hands. She reminds me about the scavenger hunt that Chris arranged for her, landing her at a restaurant where there was a bouquet of flowers waiting. She smiles as she recalls how he had all the restaurant staff in on the surprise.

"Please don't feel guilty, Gali. I know that neither of you intended to hurt the other." I pause to take a breath, tears pricking at my eyes. "You need to know how grateful I am that Chris had you in his life when he did. You played a big part in keeping him sober for those three years. He was so happy with you. Mr. McQ and I want you to know that he couldn't have had a better girlfriend as the major love of his life." I look across at her, and my tears start to fall. Chris had relapsed and started drinking after three sacred years of sobriety. This had factored into the end of their relationship. She had begun dating a guy he knew after he had decided to see other girls.

"I told myself I wasn't going to do this," I whisper.

"Me too," she says as tears slide down her cheeks. She pauses and looks me in the eye. "Thank you for bringing him into the world. I know he will always look out for me. You never forget your first love, especially when it's Chris!"

As she fills me in about school and her plans, we both relax. All I can do before I say goodbye is to let her know our family loves her and will always be here for her. As I stand up from the table, I hear Chris whisper in my ear, "Good job, Momma."

twenty

*I*n one year, from June 2010 until June 2011, while his peers were completing their junior year of high school, Chris sped through his junior and senior years. In May 2011, Joe and I traveled to Tucson for a beautiful outdoor ceremony to celebrate his high school graduation with the rest of his class in their caps and gowns. Going to In Balance Ranch Academy had made it possible for him to complete his schoolwork while he maintained his sobriety. Everyone in the audience clapped as Chris stood up to shake the owner's hand, his tanned, clean-shaven face striking. When the clapping stopped, he stood facing us from the podium and began, "How you guys doin'?" Immediately making us laugh, his low voice sped through how he'd landed at a therapeutic boarding school and his review of what he'd accomplished. "Let's see. George Patton said, 'Success is how high you bounce back when you have hit the bottom.' Through a series of unfortunate events, I was sent to Wilderness and then to In Balance, where I completed two years of high school in a single year, and now I finally feel a sense of success." He stuttered and continued, "Because of my hard work I can feel confident in my abilities, and I want to learn. Most importantly, I am now able to want more for myself and have a desire to succeed." There weren't words for the pride I felt while gazing up at my son.

A month later, when Chris completed the ranch's treatment program, I came back to town to attend another ceremony devoted to celebrating his recovery and was able to personally thank his peers and all the staff. He'd decided to stay in Arizona as part of the In Balance Transitional Living program. It was time for him to move into a group living complex in Tucson with other young men who'd already graduated. I was on top of the world. It felt like the arrival of daffodils in springtime after a tough, cold winter.

As the two of us walked outside after the celebration, Chris said, "Mom, I know I'm only seventeen, but if you sign off on it, I can get a tattoo. What do you think? There's a place not too far from here. Would you be down?" His face brightened, and he flashed a smile he knew I wouldn't be able to resist.

"Honey, you're a year sober. You've completed the program. I'll give you anything you want," I said as we walked to the car. All I was thinking about was how thankful I was that he was alive.

The next day we stood at the entrance of a little tattoo parlor off a dusty desert road. Chris pulled out of his pocket a picture of an elaborate McQuillen family crest. It didn't surprise me that he would choose a tattoo to honor his Irish heritage since he was quite proud to be a part of a big Irish family. I was surprised, however, that he came prepared. I sat next to him for hours while the tattoo artist recreated the crest on his left upper arm.

"You sure you're okay, darlin'? That's got to really hurt!" I remembered how he had once run from the doctor and hidden under her desk in another room when she was trying to give him a shot.

Chris tilted his head toward me and said, "All good, Momma." And it was. The tattoo looked as if it was meant to be there.

In the eight months since he died, numerous friends of his have been getting tattoos in Christopher's honor. I'm touched by their interest in keeping him "under their skin." I get on Facebook, and as I'm scrolling along, I see a picture of a complete replication of Chris's tattoo of the McQuillen family crest in the same location on his little brother's left upper arm. Will is too young to have done this without an adult present. How did he pull this off? I later discover he used his brother's ID. The only difference between the tattoos is the inside of the crest, where Will has his brother's initials, CJM. The caption on his post reads, "I've always wanted to be like my big bro, so I decided to get his tattoo and some detail. By the way, Mom and Dad—I got a tattoo!"

When I look at him and his tattoo, I see all the ways he is like his brother. He laughs like he did and coughs and hums under his breath the same way. He is also sensitive and sweet and not inclined to think beyond the moment he is in. He is his own person, but to the degree that he is like Chris, I can't help but be primed with the fear I could also lose him. I wish I could "un-know" that it is possible to be here one day and gone the next. I wish I could completely "un-haunt" myself.

I struggle to regain the purity of not knowing what can be lost in an instant. When my fear flares up and attaches to William, I lean on Chris to help me. When Will was young, in every picture I have of the two of them, Chris's arm is wrapped around him. Will is tucked in with a firm hold across his neck. Even after his relapse, Chris demonstrated a desire to be closer to both of his siblings and tried to be a better brother than ever. Chris came to watch Will play hockey, lacrosse, or football whenever he could. He became protective over both siblings, especially his sister. He was proud of them, even when Will achieved athletically and Caroline academically more than he had.

In the last few years, especially toward the end of his life, I saw Chris going out of his way to be there for them. Will and Chris became closer, the six-year gap between them closing in as Will seized every chance he could to be with his big brother. Will visited Chris at school, and they went to a Zac Brown concert together. Chris switched work shifts to be home for Will's birthday, and Chris posted highlights of Will's football game on Facebook: "Just my little brother being cooler than me as usual. Proud of you, bud."

When Chris died, the light in Will's blue eyes faded. He worshipped his big brother, even when there were times Chris let him down. I wish he could be restored to innocence. I know he still hears my screams in his head and that it no doubt exacerbates the sleeplessness that has already plagued him. My biggest wish for him is that someday he'll feel Christopher's spirit always looking out for him because I know he is.

With Caroline, I see evidence Chris is close at hand, guiding her in a new direction. Before he died, he came in for her sorority formal, beginning to form a friendship with her that appreciated what the two of them shared versus the ways they were different. He told his best friend he would do anything for her. She is growing beyond the drama, anger, and conflict of adolescence. I have never felt closer to this young woman whose can-do attitude, enthusiasm, and hard work amaze me.

After his graduation, Chris focused on doing his 12-step work and learning life skills like shopping, cooking, and money management. He breezed through this experience and began taking community college classes. Most boys took at least nine months to be ready to move out of the Transitional Living Program, but Chris was ready to move into a place of his own after six months. More independence was always his goal, and he went after what he wanted in his typical fast-and-furious manner.

I continued to visit Chris every six weeks. It was hard to think that his peers at home would have another year of high school filled with homecoming dances and senior year celebrations that he would miss out on. Instead, we were getting him settled into his new apartment complex. We picked out bedroom furniture together and unpacked his clothes. By just seventeen, he had already been through so much and was trying desperately to grow up. He now lived in his own apartment instead of the supervised living arrangement of Transitional Living. He shared the apartment with two other ranch graduates and had several more living close by. Chris was most excited about the pool table he and his roommates found that fit perfectly in their large garage.

Soon, Chris, one of his roommates, and another friend decided they each needed a puppy from the same litter. None of them stopped to consider the responsibility involved. Chris named his little ball of fur Sheila. She was a cuddly Australian sheepdog mix with a patch over her eye and a speckled nose. Whenever I called Chris, I'd hear him talking to her in a sweet voice without the irritability and impatience he'd so often had with his siblings. "Come on, Sheila, it's okay," he cajoled. "Noooo, no. Let's go outside. Thatta girl."

My heart leaped when I saw Christopher in a bright, emotional place. He'd become as vibrant and happy as he'd been when he was a little boy. I talked to him frequently and got pictures from him of the poker nights he and his roommates hosted at their place, all dressed up in suits and smoking cigars. Chris had stepped easily into the role of social director with his ranch friends. Joe and I relaxed into gratitude for the connection we felt with our son and for the sense of hope we could have for his future that had eluded us for so long.

For nine glorious months, from January to September of 2012, I saw Christopher emerge, as if from clay, into the best version of himself. Long neck, sharp jaw, and confidence emanating from his bright eyes. As an In Balance Ranch and Transitional Living Program graduate, he was offered the opportunity to mentor and coach the boys in treatment at the ranch. He was at his best when he could pass along what he'd learned to others, and I could sense his pride in the work he was doing. It didn't take too long for him to realize he couldn't care for Sheila due to all those hours of work. While it was hard for him to give her up, thankfully Gali's parents happily took her in.

On my visit in March, Chris took me out to the Barrasso's private ranch, where he'd been given a job working for the owner of In Balance.

"Mom, this is where we take the horses out for their exercise, here in the ring," he explained. "I'll show you." He held the lead of a chestnut brown horse and walked the large animal from the barn to the ring as I followed. I grabbed hold of the wood fence and stood on its rails as I watched him saunter toward the center of the ring. Chris had such a gentle way with animals. He looked into the horse's eyes as he patted his neck, talking to him softly. The bright sun shone off Chris's brown arms, which were still slim but more muscular from the weightlifting he'd been doing.

By then, we could spend time together with ease. My hyper-vigilance had faded. We had a routine. He'd bring a friend and come hang out at the pool of the hotel where I liked to stay, or I'd go over to his apartment. Dark brick red, radiating pale pink in the sunlight, the red, rocky mountains of Tucson became a part of him and a part of me. Chris had found friends and family here in the desert. He was at home with his "bros" and flourished in the camaraderie of his peers.

One afternoon during that same visit, I was outside cleaning up his fenced-in patio after a poker night the boys had hosted the night before. Chris called to me, "Mom, you don't have to do that! All those cigarettes! Honestly, Momma, thanks but . . ." He came outside, placed his hands on my shoulders, and guided me back indoors.

"I know, babe, but I'm here, and the guys are sleeping. I might as well help you out." I smiled sheepishly, knowing how compulsive I could be and how much I still needed to mother him any way I could.

"Come upstairs for a sec," he said as he began walking up to his room. I reluctantly left the mess and followed him. He patted his bed, indicating that I should sit down next to him, and pushed himself up against the wall. Once I sat down, he pulled a crumpled piece of lined paper out of his pocket. I saw his printed handwriting across the page. After shutting his bedroom door, he began to read what he had written.

"Dear Mom, you have always been the most loving and caring person in my life. Even when I ignored you and pushed you out of my life, you made it clear that you still loved me."

As he read on, my first inclination was to stop him. I didn't need him to apologize to me, but I knew this was important. He was making a formal amend to me as one of the steps he was working on with his sponsor, just as I'd done to my family early in sobriety and as I'd later do with him at his graveside. I knew the courage it took.

I listened attentively as he continued, "You have been supportive of my decisions and let me learn life lessons through experience. Without your constant love and support I would not be where I am today." There must have been times I thought all I needed was an apology, but in that moment, nothing mattered to me except the closeness we'd reestablished. I was so pleased about his commitment to the program. He apologized for not appreciating the love and support I'd given him while he was in the throes of his addiction and apologized for his selfishness and dishonesty. He expressed his desire to make up for his behavior. "You have a certain place in my heart. I love you and want to show you this. Sincerely, your son, Chris."

I felt as if I'd just sunk into a warm bath. The hurts of the past slipped away. I immediately wrapped him in my arms and gave him a long hug.

"My precious boy," I said as I continued to hold him tight. "There is nothing you've ever done that I haven't already forgiven you for. Thank you. You didn't have to, but thank you!"

He handed me the letter, and I could feel his relief at my proclamation of forgiveness, knowing that I wouldn't hold any of his behavior against him. My love for him had and would continue to pour out of me no matter what.

Chris celebrated two years of sobriety in May 2012, in the middle of this bright, special time, and he was reaping the rewards of his hard work. He had gotten his driver's license, and Joe was so happy that he'd bought Chris a pickup truck. He shared with us that he was struggling to manage his community college course on top of his work mentoring the boys and on the Barrasso's private ranch. We assured him he could let his class go, especially since he'd also been asked to help run groups for recovering addicts at the Tucson Ranch office. When he had time off, he took trips to California or went camping or fishing with sober friends.

One afternoon, a few months after he'd gotten the truck, I was having lunch with two girlfriends at Little Ricky's restaurant in our hometown of Winnetka when Joe called. Repeatedly. I apologized to the girls and stepped away from the table.

"Honey, what's going on?" I asked impatiently.

"Sal, I don't want you to worry, but Chris had an accident."

"WHAT? What do you mean? Is he all right?" My voice caught in my throat as I walked through the restaurant to get outside.

"He's fine. Maybe a concussion, but fine. He was driving too fast on that fricking road to the ranch with another guy, and the truck flipped. Wait, the ranch is on the other line . . . I'll call you right back."

I stood on the sidewalk, my breath escaping in puffs, impatiently waiting. My phone rang again. Joe's voice rang out as I got to my car. "He's absolutely fine. Not a scratch. The other kid sprained his wrist, but he's okay too. The ranch is telling us not to worry."

"Are you sure? There was another kid in the truck with him? Should we go out there?" I sat in my car, staring out the window but not seeing anything.

"We're lucky, Sal. The truck was totaled, and Chris came away without a scratch. God's taking care of our boy the way he took care of me!" Joe said. I shared in seeing it as a miracle, but feelings of relief eluded me. The old familiar fear slithered over my shoulder and whispered in my ear: *See? Nothing will keep him safe.* Chris had to have been driving recklessly, and while I was mad at him and knew I should be holding him more accountable, I was also so grateful he and the other boy were all right. I chose to focus on that because I needed him to be okay. My fear snuck its way back down into my chest and got hold of my lungs. Frozen, I couldn't relax in the coming weeks until I was able to get back to Tucson and see Christopher for myself. Once I was able to see him in his element and hear his stories about going to a sweat lodge with the ranch boys and holding baby wolves at a wolf rescue, fear began to loosen its grip. Chris told me he'd been asked to be the godfather to his friend Steven's new baby boy, Johnny. I could tell he hadn't skipped a beat, and it reassured me.

twenty-one

*A*t the end of that summer, Chris came home before my brother Rick's September wedding. The trees were already showing off their fall colors. Burnt red, bright orange, and golden leaves burst forth as the sun's rays lowered in the sky. Striking in his black tux, Christopher's light reflected in all our faces, evidenced by the wedding photos. To have him home so we could attend the wedding as a complete family and share in the magic of celebration with my extended family was pure joy. It was an opportunity to step outside of the day-to-day and take stock of how far Chris had come, how far we all had. Time stood still and twinkled as I basked in the feeling I'd waited for—for all to be right in my world.

After the wedding, Chris headed back home to Tucson. I got busy preparing my classroom as a preschool teacher. Having let my social work license lapse, I had been working as a substitute teacher at my children's preschool for many years. The year before, I'd taken a position as a full-time teacher to see if that was what I wanted to do.

The night before the first day of school, I was awakened by the phone ringing and looked at the clock. Midnight. When the ringing stopped, I lay my head back on the pillow. Then I realized Joe had picked up. I could hear him from our bedroom across the hall from the guestroom, where I'd sought escape from his snores.

"What?" Joe bellowed. "Where? What do you mean?"

I leaped out of bed, crossed the hall, and stood beside Joe, trying to hear what someone was saying on the other end. Joe was clutching the phone, his head down. Chris was on a trip as a mentor, taking the ranch boys hiking and camping and jumping in waterfalls through the Havasupai Indian Reservation outside the Grand Canyon.

I pieced together that he had fallen. My heart clenched. My baby was hurt. *God dammit! Not again. Oh, Christopher. What the hell now?*

Joe got off the phone and turned on the bedside lamp. The color had drained from his face. "Chris fell down an unmarked mineshaft in the middle of a cave. They've gotten him out and are heading to the hospital now." He paused, choosing his words carefully. "It was a very long fall. He's alive. They'll airlift him to Flagstaff if they determine he's not paralyzed. If they think he could be, they'll head to Las Vegas. We've got to wait to see where he'll be sent."

I stood there completely numb, refusing to absorb the possibility that Christopher might never walk again. It wasn't possible. Christopher and movement were synonymous.

For forty-five minutes, we waited. I went back to the bedroom and prayed.

Finally, we got the call. They were heading to Flagstaff. Only then did I cry the tears that had been threatening. They fell down my face as we made plans. Joe would fly out immediately. I wanted to go too but knew I couldn't. As much as it nearly killed me, I had to stay home to work and be with Caroline and William.

Our friends Michael and Melissa Sawyer lived nearby in Cave Creek. They were able to rush to the hospital in Flagstaff as Chris was being airlifted.

It felt wrong not to be there with my child. I desperately wanted to know what was happening. Instead, I showed up at work that morning with a frightened smile plastered on my face, welcoming two-year-olds to preschool. I spent the morning soothing the children after their first school drop-off, all the while dying to get an update from Joe. I tried to imagine how I might appear to the parents and staff, filling up plastic cups with primary-colored paint, setting the supplies in front of the easel, and going through the motions since I wasn't really there. My body was hovering above the classroom, drawn to my son.

The Sawyers, with their two kids Megan and Mitchell in tow, did just as Joe and I would have done had we been there. When they got to the hospital in Flagstaff, Chris was convulsing in pain. He wasn't paralyzed, but his right arm was hanging at a forty-five-degree angle, a big gash on his head had just been stitched, and his ankle was shattered.

The doctor told the Sawyers that Chris's arm would heal on its own and didn't need to be set. When the Sawyers witnessed how understaffed and chaotic the hospital was, they carried Chris to their car and raced to Scottsdale, where Michael arranged for a specialist to perform immediate surgery. From that day forward, Chris called him Uncle Mike.

By the time Joe got there, Chris had a titanium rod and screws holding his shattered ankle in place and a titanium plate keeping the bones in his arm together. He was going to be all right, but he had a long road ahead of him.

Joe spent the next week in the hospital with Chris, giving me updates while I held down the fort at home. There was an alarming bass drum solo beating in my chest, vibrating in loud,

188 ~ Sally McQuillen

unrelenting waves I couldn't get to let up, with a new crescendo of fear cresting on top.

When Chris came home a week later, he was still in excruciating pain. Joe administered pain medication shots each day. Our family room became a sick bay with crutches, a portable pee bucket, and a station for Chris's pain pills, which he insisted on taking sparingly but which he desperately needed. I made sure we monitored his meds and tried not to worry he could develop another addiction. He cried out as he attempted to get to the bathroom, but he never complained. He looked miserable in his wheelchair, and I hated that I'd not been there with him in the hospital and that I couldn't entirely be there for him now.

I taught in the mornings and rushed home to empty his bucket and bring him lunch. There were doctors and physical therapy appointments each day. We all went through the motions, strung tight. If I had permitted myself to stop and feel, anger would have had me by the throat. Burdened by my inclination to do the right thing, I hadn't left my job immediately, which I wished I had. I envied Joe for being able to be by Chris's side. If I had paused, I might have recognized that I was punishing my-self, which I have come to see as a way I've attempted to obtain control over a situation. My default being self-centered blame, I decided I had jinxed Chris by bragging to our friends a few nights before the accident about what a wild horse Chris could be, even sober. So certain that pride "goeth before the fall," I feared my pride in Chris's wildness led to this terrible incident.

Two years after his fall, when Chris was in college, he was given an assignment to write about a life-changing event.

The Day My Life Was Changed Forever
Chris McQuillen

The accident changed me forever. Even though my gratitude for life prevails, with every step I carry around the heavy weight of looking death so closely in the eyes. Two years later it is still a difficult task to attempt to travel back to that state of mind and try to explain every detail of the agony I felt in that dark pit, but the only way to rid myself of the darkness is to shine a light, which is what I will attempt to do for you and myself. . . .

When we first entered the cave, it was pretty spectacular. You could feel the history of the cave walls. As we proceeded, the cave began to close in on us. It became so dark that I could not see my hand in front of my face. I directed all the students to stop and wait for me to come to the front and see if the cave was safe to proceed any further. I slowly traversed my way to the front of the group, trying to weave my way through the students and the cave walls. Near the front of the group, I could make out Jack in the line of students. I reached my hand toward his shoulder when it happened.

BLACK OUT.

I wake up trapped in a hole of darkness. I cannot stand up or move in the slightest. I reach my left arm across my body, only to find that my right arm bone is piercing through my bicep.

BLACKOUT.

I regain consciousness without panic or worry. A feeling that I have only felt that one time sweeps over me, a feeling of contentment and serenity that I think can only be achieved when facing imminent death. I hear shouting from the students and look up to see a light coming from 55 feet above me. When I am finally able to shout back to the students, some start crying for joy, having discovered that I have not died on impact....

I had been in the cave for an hour, and I was losing blood fast. I was fully confident that the end was near. I begin to think of my family, wondering if they knew where I was and what had happened....

The narrative continued, but what would stay in my heart was this—him wondering about his family at what he assumed was the end.

Chris's fall changed things, narrowed the opening. It was far more traumatic for him than I could absorb at the time. It felt like Chris's invincibility was nearing its expiration date, and I was reckoning with my powerlessness more than ever.

While Chris was at the hospital with Joe, more of his story was revealed. Four minutes after he'd been airlifted, the sun went down, after which it would have been too dark for them to get him to the hospital. Chris even teased me about it once he got home, knowing I couldn't bear to think about it. But he hadn't shared with me that he'd had an encounter with a "stranger" who'd encouraged him to stay awake as he waited for help. I read that later. I believe this was a visit by an angel. In reading his assignment, I also found out that Chris had fallen while trying to make sure Jack, who had begun to slip, didn't fall too. I hadn't put it together that his sleep was never the same after the fall until he made note of it. It was a lot to process, but when he made light of his traumatic experience for the sake of having a good story people could laugh about later, I couldn't help but feel profound gratitude we had gotten to have him here longer.

When Chris came home to recover, In Balance owner Patrick Barrasso offered him the chance to mentor a special trip the ranch was planning to Peru in December. Chris was motivated to recover quickly. He had eight weeks to prepare. It was ambitious, but it gave him something to look forward to and go after. I wish my nerves hadn't been buzzing so loud, requiring everything I had to tamp them down. I was on autopilot. Coping by doing, I never stopped to talk to Chris about what happened and how scary it must have been.

From time to time, I'd imagine myself in the cave with Chris, but I wouldn't let myself think about the pain and fear he had endured at the bottom of that mineshaft. I locked the very idea of it away and intentionally ignored the anger that came over me whenever I thought about the mineshaft being unmarked, even after people had lost their lives. I shut out my anger over the first hospital failing him too. Instead of addressing my feelings, I ultimately left my job and put all my attention into helping Chris get well enough to climb the trails of Machu Picchu.

It's closing in on the end of September, and I'm heading back home from this morning's coffee run in my steel-colored jeep. I play a haunting song, Sheryl Crow's "Safe and Sound." It echoes all around me through collecting gray clouds. I think about how much I wanted Chris to feel like home was a safe harbor. Especially after his fall down the mineshaft. I am hurtling back in time to when it happened. It was exactly four years ago that his life changed course and ours was unsettled. September generally signals the beginning of a new school year with freshly sharpened pencils and crisp binders, with the heightened activity of back-to-school festivities, school pictures, new teachers, homework, and sports practice schedules. September began to signal when Chris's life changed course, and today, wistful remembrances turn more dramatically to burning leaves and night falling way before I want it to.

twenty-two

*O*ctober arrives, and with it, a gorgeous Indian summer. The sun dances like flames in the trees along our street. Nine months since my boy went to Heaven. I have come to believe Chris was never meant to stay. I certainly couldn't keep him here. I sit on the steps of our deck since our deck furniture has already been stored in our shed. There won't be many more days like these before the cold has me hunkering down inside.

Caroline and William are both dealing with challenges I am unable to fix, manage, or control. I am powerless to protect them from hurt and wondering how to be there for them now. Caroline is away at college; William is a senior in high school, still living under our roof. I find myself in an impotent place. Caroline has been dealing with a volatile boyfriend whom she caretakes, and William was shown a film in his health class where someone dies of drowning right before he had his lacrosse tryouts, so it was impossible for him to perform his best. This activates my trauma just as the film must have activated his. It infuriates me. I hate that my kids are facing added challenges during this tender time of grieving the loss of their brother. And I'm back to feeling like there is absolutely nothing I can do.

My role as a mother is not at all what I thought it would be. The part I'm good at is cheering for my children backstage from behind the curtains. The part that tears me up inside is when I have to watch them struggle with their parts. They each have scripts I can't dictate. At this point, I don't know what to do since it's time to stop feeding them their lines. At the very least I'd like to make sure they only have soft landings, but I know from experience that dealing with the tough stuff of life can enrich their lives and help them discover what they are made of. They now know that life isn't fair, but how can I teach them to lean into the pain, knowing how hard it is? Because through it, they will be better able to experience life's joy. They will know compassion for other people who are hurting. How can I help my children realize that it's not what happens to you but how you respond to it that builds character? I hope they will find that moving through their pain gives them an opportunity to learn what's important. I'm just beginning to figure out what this play of life is all about, and I think it might just be that we are only here on earth to grow. Being broken open can accelerate that growth.

With each passing day, there is more evidence to support what Chris has taught me. The only thing I can do is to love them. And I do. In this moment, the light in the leaves calls me from futility to hope. Chris is also teaching me that as I step further backstage, it's time to accept and love myself into becoming the main character in my own life.

I am carving out moments to pause and connect with myself and to notice how I'm feeling, asking myself what I need so I can make it a priority. Still outside on the deck, I tilt my head toward the sun as it begins to dip behind the trees, acting like Frederick from the children's book of the same name. Frederick is a little field mouse whose brothers and sisters think is lazy as they get busy collecting nuts for the upcoming long, cold winter. But all along, Frederick basks in the sun, collecting the light and absorbing the warmth of its rays, which will keep his family warm later when they must huddle together. I studied those illustrations as a little girl and remember them vividly. I visualize rays of sparkling yellow light being sent from Heaven to melt into my body. Chris's spirit is giving me access to a greater power. He has become my channel to peace. He is my oxygen mask, providing the strength and comfort to keep my heart open even when the temptation is to wall it off for protection. I know he's here with me because I hear the wind-chimes tinkling in the breeze. I close my eyes and soak up the orange glow beneath my eyelids, deciding to leave absolutely everything in God's hands and trust.

When I open my eyes and look up, I see a hawk with white-edged wings soaring in the distance. A dark dash with a flash of light comes closer, circles left, suspended above me. Then it flies further away and circles back in my direction. He flies in slow motion before heading back more quickly, each circle getting further away as if to say, "I'm here, Momma, but not for long. Look at me fly." I don't take my eyes off him until he becomes a pinprick, disappearing into thin air.

The next day I have a reading with a medium named Jill, who lives not far from NIU in Dekalb. Every medium experience is different, but I've learned to record the session or take notes because I tend to forget the details that are channeled to me. My desperation to connect with Chris makes it hard to focus.

That afternoon, pen in hand, I call Jill up on the phone and listen intently as she describes how she works. She doesn't know anything about me in advance, though I've heard from the friend who referred me to her that she is gifted. She tells me she rarely sees spirits but senses, feels, and hears them. Having said that, she stops and reports, "However, Sally, I will tell you that yesterday, I did see a young man. He appeared in my kitchen, sopping wet." I stop breathing and can't speak. She continues. "He had dirty blond hair and light eyes."

"That's my son," I whisper as my voice catches in my throat. A haunted feeling comes over me, and I attempt to concentrate. Feeling lightheaded, I listen. "This is what I am getting. He is a smart-ass, he's funny, and he has an amazing personality—so magnetic."

"Yes, that sounds just like him!" I sit up from the couch, excited.

"Oh, he is a handful. He's telling me he would do anything once. He's also a helper. A leader. He's fearless. And fun."

I've had previous readings that haven't resonated, where I've had to say, "I'm not sure what you are referring to," or "No, that doesn't really sound like him," but this is so on the money, it freaks me out. Jill has me in the palm of her hand. I scratch words across my notepad.

"He says part of him is like his dad, but that he has a lot of your qualities. His emotional side, the desire to help and heal, share, and listen. He liked to know the right thing to say or do to help the underdog. He despised bullying and didn't like it when anyone was left out."

She tells me this as if I don't already know it's true. She is getting to the heart of Christopher, having never met him. She has captured his essence, his compassion. It has all come pouring out. It makes me remember how, when Chris found out one of his fraternity brothers was back at school during break, alone on Christmas, he got up from Christmas dinner and headed back to school with a heaping plate filled with leftovers, and some presents we hastily wrapped. He showed up for friends when it mattered. Of all his qualities, it was his wide-open, eager heart that made me most proud.

She winds down the call, and I am overcome with gratitude. I feel Chris all around me. I don't know how Jill can do what she does, how any of them do. I'm not sure mediums themselves know how they connect, but Jill is a miracle worker. After thanking her profusely, she adds, "Oh, and Sally, I am not sure if this has anything to do with this reading, but this morning a big beautiful brown hawk swooped in front of my window, spread its wings, and stared at me. Does that mean anything to you?"

I lean back against the pillows on the couch and thank Chris for coming through. Amazed, I look down at my notes and imagine myself as a hawk, too, floating above my life, looking at the world from a distance. It all seems miniature. I am removed. Is this what it's like for Chris as he looks down on us from Heaven. *What's it like wherever you are, my angel?* I want to barrage him with questions. *Is it the paradise you imagined it to be? Can you see us? Hear us? Do you know what we're thinking and feeling?* I want to know and understand.

In February 2013, when Christopher was still working at the ranch as a mentor and living in Tucson, his cousin Kerry died suddenly of a brain aneurysm at the age of forty-three. She left behind her husband, Bill, and their two young sons, Ryan, six, and Alex, only two, both adopted from Korea. Kerry reveled in being a mother. She was the glue that kept us connected to all the McQuillen family in Buffalo. We were devastated.

I remember how lost my sister-in-law Pat appeared at the funeral. Joe's oldest sister, typically formidable, even intimidating to me when I'd first met her, appeared suddenly fragile. Chris flew out from Tucson for Kerry's service. As we were preparing to leave afterward, Chris sprung the news that he was going to stay in Buffalo to help Bill take care of the boys. He ended up staying for two months, essentially ill-prepared for a full-time babysitting job in the thick of family despair.

Only in retrospect do I see how losing Kerry on the heels of his fall wove more trauma into his life and set the stage for what was to come. At just nineteen, he didn't have access to the recovery support he was accustomed to in Tucson. Without his meetings, he became restless. He went back to Arizona in April but began to chomp at the bit. He decided to head to Vermont, where Sam and Zack wanted his help to promote their new band, The Dupont Brothers.

He and Sam had a special rapport. They "got each other," which was reassuring to me. I'm sure I expressed trepidation about his decision to leave the cocoon of the ranch, but there was no changing his mind. Sam and Zack would later tell me that all Chris had to do was show up and smile and their new music sold like hotcakes. I suspect that after a few months of sleeping during the day and heading to the bars to promote the band at night, Chris was feeling a bit lost. He wasn't very communicative other than to tell me how disappointed he was that Gali, who'd been planning to attend college in Vermont, was no longer able to come. At the beginning of June, Chris decided to come home to Chicago, and the guys understood.

For years after that, Sam and Zack stayed at our house whenever they drove across the country to play. Sam remained connected to Chris even when their lives went in different directions. The blending of The Dupont Brother's melodic voices was comforting, especially after Chris died. Their music will always remind me of him.

Summer arrived, and with it came my boy. His relapse had been lurking, but being home accelerated everything. Chris was immediately off to the races, trying to make up for what he'd missed. He seized every possible opportunity to party with his old friends and make new ones. Bars in the city, concerts, drinking at the beach. He told me, "Mom, maybe I can pull it off. I haven't partied since I was sixteen. I'm nineteen now, and things will be different." Oh, how I wanted to believe him. But in an instant, we were transported back to what it had been like before—and worse.

By the morning of the Fourth of July, we were a month in. Blacking out at a Jimmy Buffet concert, losing his wallet, dislocating his shoulder in a scuffle at the Pride parade. It was a familiar but accelerated roller-coaster ride. I anxiously waited for Chris to get home from being out to see fireworks the night before. He walked in the door looking tattered, his forehead gashed and bloody. He appeared pale beneath his tan. Joe told me this is what his own alcoholism was like. Messy. He told Chris too. Christopher's shame cast a dark shadow. He connected the dots and knew it was time to call it a day.

Before I could even process what happened, Chris started to pack up his stuff. Joe encouraged him to return to Arizona, knowing he would be welcomed back with open arms. And all I could feel was sad. He was leaving, and I already missed him again, even though I knew this was best. He jumped into his jeep before he could change his mind, but I could see his interest was only half-hearted. His peers were starting college, some of them landing at the University of Arizona. He just wanted to be able to do what they were doing. I understood.

Back in Arizona, Chris straddled two worlds, acting for a while like he was sober but partying with friends at U of A. From July to November, he convinced himself that he could make things work despite evidence to the contrary. There was one visit I made in October of that year where I felt really disconnected from him. He was either out with friends, or when I could pin him down, he sat with me at the hotel watching TV, not really saying much. I later realized that he had never really gotten sober after that, even though he wanted us to think he had. He came clean and admitted he wanted to attend college, too, rapidly dismissing the suggestion of attending one of the newly forming sober colleges that were popping up. His mind was made up. One of his friends lost his mother to cancer, and Chris drove all night from Tucson to Chicago to show up for him and attend her service. He didn't go back.

After being home for Thanksgiving and Christmas, Chris went on a trip to Florida with his sidekick, Cat, before getting ready for college. Cat told me later he was being "classic Chris" and that, for him, Chris was the "definition of life." There was a game out on the beach where the kids were challenging each other to swing a rope with a ring on the end of it to catch a nail. Chris advised Cat's little brother not to underestimate his opponent, "Especially if they're beautiful." Apparently, he swung and got it on his first try, announcing to the cheering crowd, "The trick is to love the game, so it loves you back."

It was amazing to have him home, and it was stressful. He started at NIU in January 2014. Admittedly I fell into despair, concerned his disease could cause him further suffering. I was afraid it would cost him. He knew I was concerned, and I knew that meant he would be more inclined to keep his partying life separate. I prayed my "Child of Light" prayer for him each morning but felt him slipping away. He was like a glorious, rare shell I might reach for in the sand as the waves pull it further from my grasp in their undertow. All I could do was trust that he would ultimately return to a sober, safer life.

I tried to detach from my worry and decelerate from my survival mode autopilot. Between my new job at the addiction center and keeping up with the comings and goings of Caroline in high school and Will in junior high, I was busy. I respected Chris's space, texting and calling just to let him know how loved he was, sometimes catching him and often not. He was fully engaged in his college life, especially once he got into his fraternity. I knew he was spending a lot of time partying, but I later found out that his college life was also full of real loyalty, love, and brotherhood with amazing friends who adored him. In the moments I miss him most, I remind myself that this chapter in his life was an incredible gift.

His friend Rommie later told me that Chris once told him he cared about three things: family, God, and friends. "But to Chris his friends were also his family." It's true. He found friends and family everywhere he went.

twenty-three

_F_all has quickly merged into winter. November, for me, prompts hibernation as the sun drops in the sky earlier and earlier. I peer out the window to watch the sun melting into smears of magenta, fuchsia, and orange dipping behind the trees. I continue to watch the sky shape-shift like the Lite-Brite toy of my childhood, setting an intention to venture beyond what feels safe, seize the moment, and carry out what I've decided is Chris's wish for me—to spread light.

Instead, I go back into the dark, familiar tunnel where I second-guess myself as his mom. I get especially tripped up around the fact that I lost him just as I'd let go of the fears I'd harbored for as long as I could remember.

Here comes the vice grip on what is left of my heart. There isn't any preparation for the experience of losing a child. All my preparing for the worst made no difference. The little girl inside me still holds the belief that if you do everything "right," there will be a good outcome, but that's not always true.

Had I stayed fearful, would it have better prepared me for what happened? No. I've concluded that fear does not serve me in any way. I am striving to fully embrace the mission of _A Course in Miracles_: to replace fear with love. Facing my fear and releasing Chris to live his life the way he wanted to was a step along this process. I know this, even if I get tripped up in thinking that letting go made my greatest fear come to pass. I can drive myself crazy, my regret manifesting in so many ways. I chew it like cud, trying to let it go until the next time I'm pulled under.

Chris's friend Sam is in town for a show a couple weeks before Thanksgiving, and we take a walk together. He asks me whether being in such grief makes me want to drink. "I'm lucky, Sam," I tell him. "Picking up a drink hasn't occurred to me. I know it would make me feel even worse." But I also confess to him that there are times I don't feel like I want to be here without Chris in this world. I rarely admit it to myself, but I need to say it out loud to someone. I have fought to stick around for Caroline, William, and Joe.

I like it when people ask me tough questions. I like going deep. It surprises me that most people I see don't ever ask how I'm feeling. I imagine it's too uncomfortable to talk about and they think they are helping by not getting into it. But if my grief isn't speakable, I feel unseen.

I especially want to be asked about Chris. I want to be able to talk about him as if he were still here. I don't want to feel like I am upsetting anyone when I mention his name. I don't want people to turn away, which they have, and I certainly don't want pity. Mostly, I don't ever want anyone to forget him. I want people to know he is around us in spirit. I want his friends to keep him in their hearts and know he is looking out for them.

Sometimes when I mention Chris's name, people look surprised and appear concerned. They don't light up when I talk about him. They shut the conversation down and say, "Of course you miss him," without saying more. I want them to say, "I miss him too. I think about him too. I get sad sometimes and remember when he was here and . . ."

If I share something about him that my friends and family have heard before, I know they are indulging me. They don't realize I cling to those stories as I won't have new ones. Instead, they turn the conversation to asking about Caroline and William. While I am happy to fill them in, too often things feel left unsaid. Too often I'm not ready to move on. I also notice that friends and family don't want to share their difficulties with me as much anymore. They assume I don't have the bandwidth or might judge their difficulties as trivial relative to mine. They might even be right, but I hope they can wait it out, as I'd hate for it to cause distance between us.

Sitting at my worn farm table desk, I'm doing homework for a course I'm taking to become a grief educator. Grief expert David Kessler makes it clear that grief is a rumination often saturated in guilt. I realize my mind often returns to that missed last chance to hug my child as he walked out the door to Wisconsin. It is one of the sharpest daggers I pull out to torture myself. One of my "if only" bargains with myself and God. My fodder for self-flagellation. But as I reflect on the teaching, I decide that Chris's hug would be all I need. It could be my fix, the ultimate fairy-tale ending. I picture wrapping my arms completely around Chris's shoulders, the scruff of his chin touching my face. I inhale his warm, smoky boy scent, kiss his head, and hold him tightly for a long time. I melt into feeling completely like myself again, my brokenness dissolving.

For this assignment we are asked to answer the following questions, "How would you revise the story of a loved one's death? How would you change a decision that went wrong?" I feel a fist smack me against my ribs as I consider how to respond. Guilt gathers in my throat and collects. I try to talk to myself as I might one of my clients, translating for them what I've learned: *Sally, guilt feelings are a way to regain a sense of control over your grief and a way to fight what is. Guilt will only cause you more suffering.* But I don't listen. I dismiss my attempts at self-compassion. The guilt gathers force and pours forth with brutality as I begin to write.

I would adamantly insist that Christopher NOT GO TO THE LAKE HOUSE. *Why didn't I tell him not to go? Why didn't I encourage him to go to the city instead? Why didn't I hug him as I always did? Whyyyyy?* I sob and sob as my heart gets shredded. I hold my breath. I am only able to write a few sentences before I have to step away.

A few days later I call my brother Rick and tell him what happened. "Usually I think I'm really doing okay, and then something crazy happens, and I realize I'm not okay. I might never be."

"Sal, what do you mean? You're doing so well," he says. "You're working so hard and . . ."

I hesitate to have my little brother think I could be falling apart, but a sob erupts. I am flooded with self-torture. I tell him how I've let go of some of my guilt, but I can't let go of the regret I feel about the day Chris walked out the door, how he was weighing his options and asked me whether he should go into the city or to the lake house. I told him the lake house sounded fun. "Oh, Ricky, I didn't tell him not to go."

"Oh, Sal." I hear him lower his voice like our dad used to when he had something important to say. "You know Chris. There wasn't a time you asked him to do something and he did it. If you asked him not to go, he very likely would have gone anyway. He was going to do what he was going to do. You're just not that powerful."

I fight back my tears enough to thank him before quickly hanging up. I walk into the bathroom and sit on the white floor tile to sob some more. I needed that reminder. It is my invitation to self-forgiveness. I'm not that powerful. I never was.

On the third weekend in November, Joe and I travel to Tucson to attend a fundraiser for In Balance Ranch. We get off the plane, and Joe looks like someone kicked him in the stomach. I keep hearing him sigh heavily as we enter the baggage claim, and I can't help but imagine Christopher walking out to greet us. He is the only reason I have ever been here. I recall how frightened we were when we dropped him off and how little we knew of what was to come. As I look out the window of our rental car, the air is thick with Chris. A part of him is imprinted in the sacred red rocks of the desert canyon. There is nothing here that doesn't make me think of him. Every mountain view, every cactus, every cowboy boot I see holds him inside it.

The grief over losing one's child never leaves you. I have lost a parent, an aunt, my grandparents, a niece, brother and sister-in-laws, and close friends. As a grief educator, I have learned that the greatest grief is always our own, and there is no ranking system for grief. But losing my son is gravely different than any other loss I have experienced. It slams me with pain coursing through every fiber of my being. In every other case, my missing of a loved one faded over time into the background of my days. But with Christopher, I don't want it to fade. Without him, I feel like I'm without myself.

I wanted to return to Arizona to remember the sacred quality time we spent here together, but I wasn't prepared to feel this desolate. I've been struck by lightning, and it crackles through me into the desert ground. We arrive at the hotel and for the first time, I hear Joe say, "It's not fair." And it's not. Chris should be here. I am not able to avoid succumbing to self-pity.

I want to howl: *Why couldn't you have stayed here in Tucson, baby? Why have other mothers' children just as reckless as mine survived? Why not you?* That night, after Joe has fallen asleep, I look out at the full moon brightly rising over the mountains and I bawl and bawl until I become parched, scraped out, bereft.

The toughest stuff of grief consists of regret, guilt, and pure pain. Grief has a mind of its own. When it comes, it hits hard. Familiar but still surprising in its power, descending as sharply as ever. Messy and unpredictable and tiring. I'm slapped in the face by its insistence. There is healing to be found in allowing the sadness of missing him to enter. It feels like loyalty. It feels like love. We are so connected that he is a part of me. I move through my pain more easily when I refrain from judging myself for it. I am dragged through its clutches, but then I come up for air and picture Christopher's green eyes smiling, giving me the strength to keep going.

The next night, I am surprised to discover that the evening is completely centered around Chris. We sit down at our table and look up to the stage where Sam Dupont begins to perform the song he wrote for Chris, ". . . reckless as those hurricane tunnels in your eyes, refused to have a bad time when you rose up out of bed, I'll be pressed to find a soul who can't admire the way you lived . . ."

Patrick Barrasso stands up on the stage to announce that his love and loss of our son prompted him to develop a charitable arm for their business. Microphone in hand, Patrick tells us how Chris would do anything for his peers at the ranch and, later, for the students he mentored and how he took the responsibility of serving very seriously. He describes how Chris drew people to him and was able to reach kids who otherwise seemed unreachable. He goes on to share how bravely Chris hiked to the summit at Machu Picchu despite the pain he was in, "driven by the opportunity to be of service to the orphans and students on the trip that needed inspiration to keep going."

Patrick then tells the audience that Chris went into shock when the pain of the descent from the summit became too great. Consistently refusing to get on the mule to make the journey easier, he pushed through the pain from his injuries and had to stop. It had gotten dark, and they were far from shelter when he stopped. Chris told everyone to go on without him, thinking he wasn't going to make it. Not just to shelter but at all.

I begin to feel faint. I had no idea. My entire body freezes as I try to take this in. I flash back to all the times I nearly lost him and try to absorb my own shock at hearing about this now. Chris had told us the descent down the mountain had been difficult. His foot had been shattered just eight weeks before, after all. He'd mentioned developing a fever but never mentioned going into shock. We'd heard only that it had been wet and cold and many of the boys got sick, but he hadn't ever told us the whole story.

When we leave the fundraiser, I turn my attention to feeling good that our son's strong spirit helped inspire the formation of this organization that will offer hope, treatment, and education to young men struggling with addiction. It is what Chris would have wanted, but I am aching as I try to process it all.

Before heading out the next day, we go to meet Chris's godson, Johnny, at the park. Four years old, he walks right into my arms and lets me hug him for the longest time, his head resting on my shoulder. I feel Chris's gentle soul inside of his and let the hot Arizona sun warm my heart as Johnny takes my hand and we walk off to feed the ducks.

twenty-four

*T*he winter holidays are upon us. This is predictably a tender emotional time. Holidays, birthdays, and anniversaries will inevitably be fraught with the agony of Christopher's absence. But there are also the unpredictable bursts of grief that send me reeling. At a recent holiday market held in a festively decorated home, I tried to tap into the magic of the season despite knowing that my feelings were raw and right on the surface. I lifted pine- and cranberry-scented candles to my nose, sampling them one at a time. Then unexpectedly, two women who are acquaintances from my community literally pulled away when they saw me. One, barely able to look me in the eye, rushed into another room and whispered to a friend. The other was clearly uncomfortable but tried to make small talk about how we both had great taste in handbags, taxing me to respond on a level so different than the one I'm in. She, too, couldn't get away from me fast enough, as if losing a child is contagious. It felt like someone left the door open and cold air blew in. I tried not to let it take me down into the darkness of my grief tunnel but had trouble shaking the way the energy changed by the backdraft I felt as they withdrew.

Shame blanketed me as I stood alone, preparing to check out, when another woman I know entered the room fresh-faced and smiling, her arms outstretched for a hug. Her brown eyes shone as she pulled me aside, saying, "I know this time of year must be especially hard for you as you miss your boy. I want you to know that you and your family are always in my prayers."

I am uplifted and wish more people could interact this way. It reassures me as I slip out the door, telling myself not to take anything personally. I try to gratefully focus on the acknowledgment of my loss I've needed, realizing I want to let go of that need. I want to grow enough so that I no longer find myself needing to be understood. I'm discovering that the most important person to acknowledge and validate my grief is me.

Not being able to bear staying home for Christmas, we head to Florida to celebrate with Marcia, her kids, and grandkids. Florida returns me to visits with my grandparents and the sticky, sweet humid air I'd breathe in immediately as I bounded off the plane. I remember Nanny and Bompa awaiting our family at the gate. Bompa, darkly tanned from playing golf. Nan, her gray bun pinned in place, a light sweater over her floral dress, waving. Our childhood spring breaks were sprinkled with Pepperidge Farm cheddar cheese goldfish placed in a fancy dish by my grandmother with a "Florida special" mixed by my grandfather with just the right amount of orange juice and ginger ale fizzing in a chilled glass. Prickly sun-burned shoulders, games of "Go Fish," and ping-pong by the pool.

On a white beach, sandpipers race back and forth on stick legs in the froth of the Gulf as the sun slips low. I walk along the ocean, scattering the sandpipers as I go, desperately searching for shells. I tell myself, *If a sand dollar appears before my eyes, I'll know you're right here,* or, *Chris, are you here? Give me a sign!* I simultaneously can't feel him and can feel him everywhere—in the shimmer of the sun, the whisper of the wind, the laughter I hear as children play.

As I make footprints in the sand, I picture myself on a boat, kneeling against the wind, head craned out over the ocean. The sky has streaks of gold running through it, reminiscent of the orange sunsets I observe in some of the shells I've collected. God, I love a boat. I'd forgotten the peace of the wide-open sky above me and the water below. The familiarity of the mangroves, the inlets, the gulls. I especially love the feel of a boat racing along, the sea splashing over the bow in an arc. I've come back to myself. Christopher is with me. I'm lighter and restored.

But then I go from elation to fright in the span of one second. The four of us are out for dinner at a local restaurant that evening, and I reach for my necklace only to discover that my neck is bare. My Tree of Life is gone. I keep grasping at my neck to locate its branches.

Caroline and Will see me freeze. "Mom, what's wrong?"

"Momma, you, okay?"

I can't speak. I tell them I'll be right back and race outside to the car, Joe following me. I search everywhere—under my car seat, in my shawl, on the restaurant's bathroom floor. But I know it's gone. Just as I'd known my son was. The absence of its weight against my skin triggers an all-too-familiar yearning in my chest. I get swept away, overcome, realizing I had been pulling at my necklace during my beach walk earlier. Intent on my hunt and thinking of Christopher while keeping my eyes peeled for rare shells, my necklace must have slipped into the fine stretches of sand.

After dinner, beside myself, I return to the beach, walking where I'd walked earlier. I'm in a state of futility as I enter the water straight toward the night, heading for the rising surf under the moon's glow, thinking I might just keep walking. Deeper and deeper, I could just go. Find my boy.

The waves catch the light as I cry without making a sound. I seek the comfort of my son and search for him in the stars above.

"Are you there? I've lost you. I've lost your last gift to me." I stand in the moonlight, the sea up to my thighs, when I hear him reassure me.

"I'll never be lost to you, Momma. You no longer need the strength your necklace gave you. Nothing can take me from you." I feel him wrapping his arms around me, accepting that my necklace has become a buried treasure and is where it is meant to be. More letting go. With a final sigh, I thank Chris and the darkening sky and walk back to where Joe, Caroline, and William are waiting.

The next day I don't go in search of perfectly shaped shells whose names Nanny would whisper in my ear: Olives, coquinas, cat's eyes, lady's slippers, Japanese hats, and turkey wings. This time, as the waves tug at the shore, I gravitate to the shells bleached by the sun and barraged by the sea. With their lines and holes, they are beautifully battered. Lifting clumps of seaweed from the sand, I spot the whelks and scallops still clinging. I peel them off, admiring their colors and design, and hold them tightly in my palm.

As I study their pale orange, gray, bright pink, and soft browns and add them to my collection, I relate to them. These shells and I have housed living creatures inside us, tried to protect them, and been whittled by the waves. I am fascinated by their shapes and how they came to be. I have researched how shells are formed and discovered that the materials creatures absorb from the ocean harden in layers to become their homes. I've read about how when a creature dies or outgrows its shell, its exoskeleton is left behind to wash up on the shore. Losing my Tree of Life necklace has also left me feeling washed up and left behind.

Yet, when I pick up shells and dip them in water to release the sand, they shine. I am soothed as I rub their softened edges between my finger and thumb. I think about how their creatures go on to find new shells after they let go and how new chapters begin for all of us.

The waves crash, creep closer, and retreat. I talk to Chris, my words floating in the warm breeze. I feel the sun brown my skin as I inhale the crisp scent of the ocean. I watch for dolphins and continue to be lulled by the sweep of the tide as it goes in and out. I find myself in a watercolor of scalloped white waves as the turquoise-green water sprays against the sand. I pause and look down, and at my feet above my toes lies a bright white perfect sand dollar.

This becomes my new Tree of Life. Broken open, fragments shaped like doves make it a token of peace. When I get back from my walk, I look up the spiritual meaning of sand dollars and read about how the five small holes at each point represent Christ's wounds and that sand dollars are talismans for those going through transformation beyond suffering. That afternoon, Joe and I go for a drive to Saint Armand's Circle and stop at a little jewelry shop. Lo and behold, the owner has designed his own gold sand dollar pendants. The star pattern embedded on top helps me know it is a gift from Christopher from the sea.

Back home, it is January 3, 2017. The one-year anniversary of the day my son did not come home. Time has no meaning. I may as well have lost him yesterday or a million years ago. I light a candle and thank Christopher for all the gifts he brings. *Thank you, my gorgeous boy, for helping me cut through all of life's most difficult moments to keep my eye on the prize. To seize opportunities to give love at every opportunity. Just as you did.* I hope, as I gain solid footing, that I will be able to put myself out there in the world more and live life as fully as Chris did in his twenty-one years on earth.

Today, Joe grieves Christopher just as he has been. His grief is loud and overpowering, just like his love. He gets flooded with emotion, his tears stream out from his eyes, and his tough Irish face becomes a sponge, squeezing out more. I hear him stomping up the stairs and greet him upon his return from the grave. He drops the top of his head toward me for me to pat before giving him a hug, knowing that once he is home his sadness will overtake him. Our pain is shared. Only Joe loves Chris as fiercely as I do. And yet we grieve alone and differently. My grief is intimate and sacred. I prefer to retreat to a quiet place to cry or to write directly to Chris rather than expose the inner linings of my heart.

At the same time, I want everyone to know that I miss everything about him with every fiber of my being. He is one of the best things I ever did. There is simply no one anything like him, no one so alive. I want everyone who never had the chance to meet him to feel his spirit lift them up. I want to show him off. I write a tribute to him to honor him, crawl under the covers, and look back through Chris's social media posts to help me feel his energy.

When he took off with his friend Brian from their adventure in New Orleans to Florida to "supervise" high schoolers on the beach, he posted, "Well, this is impulsive." It certainly was. Or "I am at a crossroads in my life" when he couldn't decide which Buffalo Bills jersey to buy. "Best Day of the Year" for St. Patrick's Day. No surprise there. And then I see what he posted before our last Christmas together: "Christmas always reminds me how lucky I am. An amazing loving family at home, friends from home who I have grown up with and would kill for, and the best brotherhood a man could ask for. Thank you all."

I locate his tweets. It looks like he was on Twitter in November and December before he died. They bring him to life.

"Two of my favorite things in the world: my mom and my dog."

"Bruh all I need is a beach and a book."

"Life is honestly so beautiful as long as you allow it to be."

"Family first no matter what."

"What a beautiful god damn day."

Nobody scratches the surface of Chris. Alternatively deep and wise and hilariously himself, he continues to amaze me. As I carry on, I welcome the moments when his presence is undeniable. I am moving from looking for evidence of him everywhere to believing he's with me even if I can't lay my eyes on him. I will choose gratitude, knowing that I got to be his mom and still get to be his mom always. I will choose the joy his bright spirit makes me feel instead of feeling sorry for myself. I will spend the rest of my life trying to make him proud.

I often try to tap into a sense that all is well even when it doesn't feel like it and all I can touch is my unrest. I work to adapt to my new reality and accept that Chris is no longer here in physical form. When I focus only on my ongoing crush on my firstborn, light breaks through my darkness. I think back to sitting next to Monika on the plane heading to Savannah when we talked about *A Course in Miracles*. It was Chris's way of giving me access to a fresh way to see. Since studying the daily lessons, I am welcoming more moments of peace and safety. I am choosing and changing how I perceive the world and finding comfort where I can. It's not that I don't feel pain, but when I am consciously trying to turn away from the darkness of the fear that compounds it, the pain shifts. When I place my pain at the altar of my love, light softens it.

Examining fear head-on as part of my grief process, I have decided it no longer serves me, and I pray I can outgrow it. All the extreme feelings like fear and love that exist within grief make it complex to process and understand. The fog and clarity, devastation and joy, security and groundlessness, vulnerability and resistance, struggle and peace, terror and courage, self-pity and gratitude, guilt and forgiveness. Indefinitely. Both. And. Grief holds it all.

My love for Christopher continues to build. It flows out for him and never stops. It rolls, it flies, it accelerates and expands, bursts and climbs. It hugs. And it gives me purpose. I am forming a new understanding of why I am here and what I am meant to do on Earth while Chris is in Heaven. To me, he hasn't died. His spirit sits on my shoulder as I find meaning in my work as a therapist, joy in being a mom to Caroline and William, and continued love from him as I show up in the lives of his friends to celebrate their milestones, just as he would have.

It's like being in an airplane looking out the window. As we approach the dark gray clouds of suffering, where I so easily go, I feel my ego's self-centered insistence that things should be different than they are. I fight what is, wishing Chris could be alive again. I experience guilt, self-pity, and fear in the swirling mist and press my palm against the glass. The plane is spinning. I get sucked into a vacuum of emptiness, lost in the underbelly of the clouds where I couldn't save him. I can't see clearly.

But then the plane ascends, and the darkness evaporates. The clouds are haloed in pale pink light. I move away from the despair calling me toward it into peace. Christopher takes my hand and guides me higher beyond the puffs of white into the brightest deep blue sky where the sun shines upon my face.

Seven more months pass, and we are nearing the end of summer. I listen as Christopher encourages me to head to the north woods, where there is a serene, wooded world of nature that will ground me. I drive up to Grammy and RaRa's cabin, stumbling onto the fact that the Perseid meteor shower is currently at its peak, so if I'm lucky I will get eyes full of shooting stars.

I'm here at their home in the woods. Earlier tonight I thought I heard something and stopped in my tracks. I shone the light from my phone into the trees, but there was nothing I could see. I sat on the stone steps near the driveway, listening. I took some deep, conscious breaths, letting stillness wash over me. Then something strange happened. It sounded like a woman crying. Deep and pained. But it couldn't have been. Any of the few neighbors across the lake would have been sound asleep. Was I imagining it? Was it the cry of a mother who lost her child? Was it a coyote wailing? Or was it my own yearning to connect to Chris finding its voice? I listened closely and heard several more crying pleas followed by complete quiet.

When my alarm goes off later that night at 2 a.m., I feel a tingle of excitement. I find my way down the mossy path through the trees down to the lake. A breeze stirs and makes the water beneath the dock gurgle. A fish jumps, or a frog hops, and then quiet returns. I turn off my flashlight and look up.

Greeting me is the most incredible sight. Hundreds and hundreds of stars beckon me out to the end of the dock. I feel so small and alone, but not alone. As I detect the ambient sound of a cricket's whir, I drop into a chair. The stars reveal themselves in outbreaks of light, and Chris reveals himself too. I sit back, absorbing the realization that the stars are always there—we just can't always see them. I soak in their twinkling as if I'm falling backward. I ask myself whether this might be what it feels like to die. To feel like a star swallowed by the night, drawn into an infinite galaxy of beauty. My soul lifting out of my body, leaving this self-centered human existence behind as I soar toward the vast source of light where my son lives.

There are so many stars that constellations aren't identifiable. No Big and Little Dipper, no North Star. When I contemplate what it's like to be human, I picture us as stars smeared together in the Milky Way. Our experience universal, we are all connected. I am lost in a smattering of stars overlaid by wispy watercolor clouds sprinkled with more stars.

I wait for the meteors to fall, feet from where Chris long ago stood catching a little fish. Out of the corner of my eye, a horizontal streak of light moves from left to right across the lake. In turn, a zip of light streams from right to left above the forest. Mesmerized, my neck tightens up and my throat becomes dry. Hungry for more flashes of Chris, I stand up from the chair, raise my arms up high, and reach for the beautiful sky.

At that exact moment I call out, "I love you, Christopher!" Three more stars shoot simultaneously in various directions, dancing through the darkness, their white tails burning brightly. I hold my eyes shut, trying to lock the feeling of his spirit close into place, but the flashes last only seconds and are gone.

Sally and Chris
photo courtesy of the author

afterword

*I*t took me seven years to write *Reaching for Beautiful*, which I condensed into the first year of my grief journey. And it took me seven years, four months, and nineteen days after losing Christopher to start to feel like myself again. I want to normalize the fact that the grief process for those suffering the loss of a child lasts a lifetime. My acute early grief lasted at least four years even though, to the outside world, I appeared to be functioning. The third year I cried nearly every day with few exceptions. The first two years I cried every day, endlessly surrendering to waves of sorrow or bracing against them.

For as long as I'm alive, I have no doubt that I will periodically be ambushed by an overpowering yearning. I will descend into an excruciating ache I couldn't have fathomed before my heart was struck. But I will do my best to welcome grief when it overtakes me, as it is an outlet for my affection and boundless love for my boy. It reminds me that Christopher's absence on this earth cannot ever—will not ever—be filled. I know that I will miss him many moments of every day, and I wouldn't have it any other way.

Since my grief is now more integrated, its gifts are rising to meet me. I have come back home to myself stronger. With the

222

consolation that my son's spirit is fueling me at my core, I no longer think of him as out of reach. He inspires me to go beyond the limits of fear toward love multiplied. I feel him with me often, especially when I'm in awe of nature's beauty. It's as if I'm looking at his beautiful face when the sun's bright rays break out from a cloud-filled sky, giving him a hug when a soft, warm breeze gently finds me, or listening to his voice when light dances playfully on the water.

resources

GRIEF ORGANIZATIONS

Helping Parents Heal is a non-profit organization dedicated to assisting parents whose children have passed. Through support and resources, they aspire to help individuals become "Shining Light Parents," meaning a shift from a state of emotional heaviness to hopefulness and greater peace of mind.

Helpingparentsheal.org

The Compassionate Friends organization provides highly personal comfort, hope, and support to every family that has experienced the death of a child, sibling, or grandchild, and helps others better assist the grieving family.

Compassionatefriends.org

The MISS Foundation website provides quick access to counseling resources, advocacy information, research on traumatic grief, education for healthcare providers and community members, and support services for those grieving the death, or impending death, of a child.

Missfoundation.org

Grief.com is dedicated to helping everyone deal with the often unknown terrain that comes along with all kinds of grief through education, information, and other helpful resources to make the challenging road of grief a little easier.

Modernloss.com is a place to share the unspeakably taboo, unbelievably hilarious, and unexpectedly beautiful terrain of navigating your life after a death.

OptionB.org

STAND-OUT BOOKS ON GRIEF

The Year of Magical Thinking by Joan Didion

A Grief Observed by C.S. Lewis

Man's Search for Meaning by Victor E. Frankl

It's OK That You're Not OK by Megan Devine

Anxiety: The Missing Stage of Grief by Claire Bidwell Smith

On Grief and Grieving by Elizabeth Kubler-Ross and David Kessler

Finding Meaning by David Kessler

The Wisdom of Grief by Leslie Palumbo

Option B by Sheryl Sandberg and Adam Grant

My Search for Christopher on the Other Side by Joe McQuillen

We're Not Done Yet, Pop by Joe McQuillen

Lament for a Son by Nicholas Wolterstorff

Healing After Loss by Martha Whitmore Hickman

acknowledgments

To my immediate family—you give my life its deepest meaning. Joey—Bear, our whole is greater than the sum of its yin and yang parts. Your energy, hard work, faith, and conviction inspire me. Thank you for being my partner in this life, and thank you for keeping me laughing. Chris would say he couldn't have asked for a better dad who dropped everything every time to be there for him.

Caroline—Moma, you are my favorite girl, and you rule my world. I'd go anywhere with you. I'm amazed by the force of your nature. Thank you for being my daughter and best friend. Chris wants you to know he is by your side, forever taking seriously his big brother role to keep you protected. And to your fiancé Paul, our chill, tall tree, I knew you were the one. And Lovie, for the joy you and your heart-shaped pink nose bring our family.

William—Bugs, there is nothing I wouldn't do for my "baby." You make my life complete and so much better. You truly are the icing on our family cake. Thank you for allowing me to hug you as much as I want. Chris wants you to know he will keep cheering for you on the sidelines and loves you more than you could ever know. And to your girlfriend Linnea, our mountain girl, you are the flowers on top of the icing.

To the McQuillen family—for rallying to no end as a team I'm proud to be a part of. Go Bills!

Specifically, I want to express love and gratitude to the family members I envision greeting Chris with a party when he arrived in Heaven—his cousin Kerry, Grandmother Rita,

Grandpa Joe, Aunts Pat and Diane, and Uncles Jerry, Billy, and Bobby. To his godmother, Aunt Marcia, whose love sparkled over us all. Chris was proud to be a McQuillen and adored his Aunts Maureen, Linda, Kathy, and Debbie, his Uncles Paul, Bill, and Tom, and his many cousins and their spouses. He loved his cousins-once-removed with his whole heart—Evan, Kate, Bridget, Ryan, Alex, David, Matthew, John, Claire, Elizabeth, Zach, Mary, William, Eliza, Megan, Steven, Mark, Kara, Jamie, Patrick, Matthew, and Sarah.

To my side of the family—for showing up immediately. I want to thank my mom, Mary, Chris's grandmother (Grammy), stepdad Bud, grandfather (RaRa, the name Chris gave him), my brother Charlie and sister-in-law Carolyn, brother Rick and sister-in-law Perrin, niece Emma, brother Douglas and sister-in-law Carmela, sister Christina and brother-in-law John, and niece Genevieve. I adore my goddaughters Emilie and Katie, my nieces Wynter, Marion, Alice, Chandler, and Ashley, my nephews Andrew, Jacob, Scottie, Charlie, and Stephen, and my cousin and sister Anne. And I'm thankful for Uncle Dick, Aunt Carol, cousins David, Steven, and Jeffrey, my half-brother Nicholas, stepmom Susanne, my stepbrothers Greg and Steve, their wives, Kimberly and Wendy, and their sons, Grant, Hayden, Jack, Will, and Paul. Chris loves you and thanks you all for taking care of his momma.

A special thank you to my grandmother Nanny, grandfather Bompa, and godmother Aunt Eda, whose love from above has offered great comfort. And a nod of gratitude to my beloved Cassidy, whose softest ear and companionship are deeply missed.

To the many folks in our community, including those who have lost children of their own, to the strangers we'd never met, who brought us pots of soup, warm cookies in baskets, and armloads of flowers—every kind gesture, card, and gift carried us.

Extra gratitude goes out to all the friends and family who flew in from out of town to be with us immediately after our world was rocked. To Amy Zeh, Casey Tomassene, Sheila Kane, and Ina Sherman, your friendship will never be forgotten. To my dearest friends for always, Robin McKinney, Debbie Retondo, Lisa Mathias, Laura Dunbar, Cammie Naylor, Ellen Heaney, Cathy Drechsler, Annie Fitzpatrick, Wendy Stevens, and Alyson Minkus. To include my writing group friends, without whose writing wisdom, ongoing encouragement, and feedback I could not have completed this memoir. Our friendship is sealed for life, Julie Fingersh, Kristen Moeller, and Brenda Wilkins. And to my many pals who have a special place in my heart, even if I don't get to see your faces as much as I'd like, to include Julie Feeney, Cindy Brady, Tane Beacham, and Maureen Noble.

Thank you to my therapist, Ellen Katz, for nurturing and challenging me and to my twelve-step community for being open-armed and willing to witness, and thank you to my sponsor for facilitating self-forgiveness. And I want to give a huge shout-out to all my clients who grant me the privilege of their trust. I love you all.

I'd also like to thank my high school humanities teacher, Barbara Anderson, and my advisor and college writing professor, Tony Stoneburner, for stimulating my love for writing. Thank you to the writers Laura Munson, Lisa Jones, and Bridget Boland for their hand in my memoir. An extra hurrah goes out to my editing coach and publisher of She Writes Press, Brooke Warner, editing coach extraordinaire, with whom everything felt secure and remarkably fell into place. Thank you to Jill Maxick at PR by the Book for helping me share my story. My appreciation goes out to beta readers Rick Stearns, my brother and confidante, and Lonnie Stonitsch, Executive Director of Family

Action Network, and bestselling author, Sukey Forbes, for their time and insight.

Thank you to Vera Pekic, the Barrasso Family, the Sawyer Family, Kim Jenkins, Thad Ryan, Ben Pearson, Steve Schaecher, all the moms who loved Christopher, and the teachers who supported him, for your roles in caring for my boy. It does take a village.

To Chris's friends from childhood, from home, from In Balance Ranch, his friends and brothers from AKL at NIU, and the many others he made near and far who love him still that I may have failed to include—may you feel his ineffable spirit with you always.

James B., Sean S., Isaac D., Sam C., Jeff C., Campbell L., Connor H., Jack K., Nick D., Nick H., Nathan C., Mac F., Seamus H., Nick C. (Cat), Rommie K., Jimmy C., Jack C., Justin H., Emma H., Scottie B., Brian G., Patrick O., Pat W., Brian H., Will C., Daniel S., Ted L., Joey P., Sam K., Cam K., Grant S., Tyler R., Taylor S., Avery H., Lyndsey H., Gali A., Claire C., Sydney J., Elly G., Jessie P., Hilary H., Hanna S., Clair M., Emily K., Izzy P., Sarah B., Danny Z., Carla Z., Glory G., Corey H., Sean K., Josh S., Chris L., Chris C., Conor G., Wyatt H., Henry S., Eric F., Sam D., Zack D., Dom, Joe C., Steven G., Matt T., Pierce B., Max R., Nicky M., Chase B., Mitchell H., Jason T., Jeff G., Jeff S., Sean D., Adam K., Mish, Samantha B., Nick T. (Tommy), Surry, Raul E., Bryan C. (BCass), Ryan B. (Bailey), Ben E., Brad P., Liam R., Sarah M., Robyn Y., Kari A., Gina P., Maggie R., Alyx C., Victoria F., Kevin F., Alejandro C., Zach H., Patrick M., Bryan L. (BLo), Francisco R., William H., Eric P., Eric J., Zach B., Zack M., Rich B., Brian C., Tim A., Parker F., Mark C., Jason B., Evan H., Matt C., Matt S., Justin G., Mauricio C., Mike H., Anja C., Kiran P., Donna B., Jessie E., Louis G., Brandon P., Ricky M., Janar N., Nicky M., Luis M.,

Austin R., Wes C., Aaron O., Stephen P., Tommy D., RJ B., Taylor D., Kelly B., Ted L., Ryne D., Brandon V., Chris K., and John D.

Thank you to my readers for staying the course. I know this isn't the easiest of reads. I hope if you are a grieving parent, reading this book helped you feel less alone. My heart is with you.

To those mothers raising a wild child of their own, sending you hugs and the stamina to keep up.

And to those of you who didn't get the chance to meet Chris, I hope this book helped you feel like you know him so you could experience a hit of his light.

about the author

Sally McQuillen, LCSW, CADC, is a psychotherapist in private practice specializing in addiction, grief, and trauma recovery. An avid reader with a double major in writing and dance criticism in college, she began working in public relations and marketing prior to obtaining her master's degree in social work. She and her husband live on the north shore of Chicago where they raised their three children. *Reaching for Beautiful* is Sally's first book.

Looking for your next great read?

We can help!

Visit www.shewritespress.com/next-read
or scan the QR code below for a list
of our recommended titles.

She Writes Press is an award-winning
independent publishing company founded to
serve women writers everywhere.